Earth to God, Come In Please...

Available from ECKANKAR

This book has been reviewed and published under the supervision of the Living ECK Master, Sri Harold Klemp.

Earth to God, Come In Please...

ECKANKAR
Minneapolis, MN

Earth to God, Come in Please . . .

Compiled by Suzanne Ford
Edited by Joan Klemp
Anthony Moore
Mary Carroll Moore

Text and cover illustrations by Fraser MacDonald

Second Printing—1994

Earth to God, come in please—/ [compiled by Suzanne Ford].
p. cm.
Preasssigned LCCN: 91-70353
ISBN 1-57043-053-5

1. Eckankar (Organization) 2. Spiritual life—Eckankar (Organization) I. Ford, Suzanne Alexander.

BP605.E3E17 1994   299'.93
                                               QBI94-1577

Contents

Introduction

The Voice of God resonates through all creation. The shepherd Moses heard and saw It in the burning bush while on the mountaintop. The ancients harkened to the sacred oracles. But how does the Voice of God speak to the space age?

How do we get answers to our heartfelt questions— answers that come not from faith or wishful thinking, but from direct experience and knowing?

The stories in this book are a collection primarily from the annual magazine, the *ECKANKAR Journal* (formerly the *ECK Mata Journal*). These stories share life-changing experiences and insights of people who are searching for the deepest purposes of life.

These people are from every walk of life. Each one has embarked on what might be called a spiritual research project. Through their study and practice of unique contemplative exercises, they have learned that within the ordinary events of life, *extra*ordinary insights and lessons can be found.

The exercises and principles in the teachings of Eckankar helped the authors of these stories find a greater purpose for their lives. How? By revealing simple ways to tap their inner wisdom to bring them more freedom and love.

One woman shares how a prophetic dream helped her prepare for her new job. Another relates her view of why we have difficult experiences—and how to get the most from them. A third story by a man from Hong Kong gives an unusual technique to quit smoking.

You'll read about the experiences of a man who was able to gently escort his father beyond the veil of death and into the arms of a spiritual guide. A woman who lost a child was able to prove for herself that Soul is immortal. Her story reveals how she discovered her baby had reincarnated as another son. Other stories share dreams of prophecy, past-life remembrances, miraculous healings, and startling meetings with remarkable Adepts.

As you read, you can experiment with the unique visualizations, attitudes, and approaches shared by the authors. If you work with them daily, they can expand your awareness of how life works. These methods range from keeping a journal of your dreams to fine-tuning your intuition, from singing a special word that opens your heart to God's love to watching how your pet teaches you.

This book would not be possible without the spiritual insights and exercises provided by Harold Klemp, the current leader of Eckankar. The end goal of any spiritual search is to gain self-mastery. The tellers of these stories have found that a teacher—one who is adept at serving as an inner and outer guide—can offer many shortcuts to this goal. The teachings of Eckankar have helped them gain more direct awareness of their own inner guidance.

The rewards of listening to your inner guidance are great. Like the people you'll meet in these pages, you can start living the life you were born to lead—filled with rich meaning, love, and trust in the greater purpose at work in your daily experiences.

1
Past Lives
and Reincarnation

We've all lived in other times and places.

Checkers

Doug Culliford

One child was six, and the other three. It was a preholiday gathering of family, and someone popped the question:

"What do you want for Christmas?"

"Checkers," replied the six-year-old girl. "I want checkers for Christmas."

"Checkers! Why, you don't even know how to play the game."

"Yes, I do!" the little girl replied sharply.

"Who taught you how to play checkers? Did you learn in school? Did your parents teach you?"

"Nobody did. We always used to play checkers." The girl's eyes were mirrors of truth.

"You and who else?" someone asked.

"My brother and I." The three-year-old brother looked up and nodded agreement to the questioning adults. "We used to play before, when we were big."

"Before? When was that?"

"When we were big before. Before we came to live here. We were old, older than you."

One adult consulted another. Minutes later, an old, dusty box of checkers was found and set up in front of the two children. Sure enough, the moves were familiar to them. The puzzled adults looked on as the brother and sister moved pieces nimbly around the board.

"Did you live together before?" someone asked.

The little boy kept on playing, letting his older sister do the talking. "My brother and I lived in the same house then. We were married."

Someone mentioned a deceased uncle. The little girl piped up, "I knew him too! I met him before I came here to live with you!" This uncle had died before the six-year-old was born, and the doubting adults shook their heads at her fantasy. But she went on to describe him perfectly.

The curious thing was, this family held to a particular religion which didn't acknowledge reincarnation. But over the years the family had had many mysterious encounters with deceased relatives. Bit by bit, they crossed the fine line between religious doctrine and actual spiritual experience. They began to acknowledge, through their certainty of these experiences, that reincarnation was not only possible, but probable. And they moved one step further from their limitations and one step closer to spiritual freedom.

Dreaming My Life

Denise Naughton

Although dreams have always brought me spiritual insights, there are very few dreams I remember from my childhood. The ones I do remember woke me in the middle of the night, frozen with fear. Only the sound of my racing heart broke the silence.

These nightmares were very rare and always the same: My house was surrounded by Japanese warriors. I was the only defender against the onslaught of dozens. I would wake in a cold sweat just before they made their rush.

As I grew older, these dreams disappeared. But the key to unlocking their meaning surfaced years later in a love relationship.

From the beginning of our relationship, my partner and I enjoyed the easy familiarity of old friends. I remember once he mentioned he had known me a very long time ago. "How wonderful it is to be with you again," he said. I was taken aback by his comment. It was out of the ordinary for him and out of context with the conversation we were having.

I tried to quiz him, but he couldn't explain it. He

seemed rather confused by what he had said. I knew it was a message from Divine Spirit, and I listened.

Our relationship was an unusual one. Everything seemed to indicate it would be long and full. However, we would reach a certain point and then, for no apparent reason, back away from each other. Every two to three years we reconnected, only to reach the same barrier again. This pattern repeated itself for almost twelve years.

During the years we were apart, our relationship continued in the dream state. My family and several of the ECK Masters of the Ancient Order of the Vairagi played a part in these dreams. My family was always confused: Why was I leaving such a wonderful man?

In other dreams our relationship grew in the ways I had always expected it to in my outer life. I was becoming very confused. Outwardly the relationship was going nowhere, but it was working so well on the inner!

One time after spending a few days with him, I returned home feeling inwardly beaten and broken. Once again the wall of fear had reappeared. It reminded me of my childhood nightmares. A decision needed to be made: either I wanted us to be together completely—or not at all. But I was paralyzed. I couldn't decide what to do next.

I sat down and did a spiritual exercise to gain some insight into my fear and confusion. I asked the Mahanta, the Inner Master, to show me why I could neither shake this bond nor make it stronger. Then I fell asleep, and my dreams brought me the answers I sought.

In a dream that night I found myself in Japan. The setting was several centuries ago. I saw a woman and a man, both dressed in royal robes, their families attending. At first I thought I was watching a royal marriage, but then I realized the two were being slowly tortured.

Why? I knew I was the woman, but who was this man? Someone urged me to move closer and to be silent; the answers would come. Suddenly I found myself in the body of the woman I had been watching. My father was commanding me to deny the love I had for the man by my side. I asked him why. He replied that this man was the enemy of our family.

I replied he was no enemy of mine and turned to look into my lover's eyes. It was then that I recognized him as the man I knew in my present life. In this past life in Japan, he and I had died at a very young age at the hands of our own fathers. They had been lifelong enemies, coming together briefly for the murder of their only children.

When I awoke, I knew I had experienced a past life as Soul. All my childhood nightmares now made sense. Those fears were gone—and with them, the bond with this man. I understood from the dream that our relationship could go no further in this lifetime. He would not be able to understand the obstacles we would have to overcome to renew our relationship as it was in that past life. But instead of feeling sorrow, I felt light and happy. I was walking away from this relationship with love, understanding why rather than resenting invisible circumstances.

Someday, I knew, this man and I would meet again on equal ground. This was the insight from my dream: that there is a love that is greater, freer, and stronger than the love I was familiar with in the physical world. I could leave our relationship with love and know that it was still being healed on the inner planes.

Though the outcome of the relationship was not what I had visualized and hoped for, the ECK, or Holy

Spirit, had give me something better: an open heart and an understanding I could carry with me forever.

Connections of the Heart

Coleen Morimitsu

The Eckankar Satsang class closed with a hushed HU-U-U, a moment of silence, then smiles everywhere. A tangible glow hung in the air. Through my peripheral vision, white light twinkled around each student. I wanted the moment to last forever.

People milled about the room, reluctant to depart. A group congregated near the door, trading hugs as they left. I quietly slipped into the outer foyer to be alone.

I saw another chela, a student of Eckankar—a person I'd spoken to barely half-a-dozen times before. Shyly, I glanced at him as laughter from the other room trickled and spilled over us like water. His eyes met mine and a slow smile passed between us. Simultaneously, we laughed and shrugged, as if to say, Why not?

I extended my arms to him as he stooped slightly to surround me in a gentle hug. Closing my eyes as his arms clasped around me, I felt my heart open with a flood of warm light. I sensed his heart was open too, and it was as big as all outdoors.

Instantly, I saw a woman I knew to be myself, standing in an open meadow in front of a weather-beaten farmhouse. A prairie wind whipped her skirts as she gazed across distant fields, searching for the man she loved. A flash of recognition crossed her face. Her wrinkles of worry melted into a smile as she ran into the arms of her husband. The warmth of their love enveloped them as they embraced.

As the vision faded from my inner eyes, I still felt those strong arms, wrapped with love around the prairie woman. With a start I realized—I knew this Soul! This was the man from the field. He was so familiar. I was struck wordless by the sacredness of the moment.

Slowly I grasped his shoulders and gazed into his soft, brown eyes. As he gazed back, I glimpsed something I'd seen in the eyes of wild animals. Pure ECK shone there, full of tenderness, trust, and the light of love. My breath caught in my throat. Tears sprang to my eyes as Soul acknowledged Soul. My heart overflowed with love.

"Get to know this chela better," I heard the voice of the Inner Master request. Dimly, I heard the chela ask, "I'm going to grab a bite to eat. Care to join me?"

Inwardly I debated. I wanted to listen to the Inner Master, but my ego fought for control. Incredulously, I heard my voice stammer out an apology. "Thanks, but some other time, maybe." Ego felt I wasn't ready for this experience. It wanted time to prepare—for me to be at my best.

Again, more insistently, I heard the Inner Master. "Get to know this chela, *now!*"

"I will, I will," I promised inwardly. "Later, just not right now." I turned hesitantly toward my car. An inner pull begged me to turn back. I stopped to look back, all the while inwardly kicking myself. Five minutes later, I found myself on the freeway, speeding home.

Days turned to weeks, and the weeks began to slip by, stacking into months. Still, my promise remained unfulfilled each time I saw the chela. Each time the Inner Master admonished, "There isn't much time. Get to know this chela."

Surely there must be plenty of time, I reasoned. Incredibly, I found myself arguing—yes, debating with the Inner Master. I finally decided that at the ECK Regional Seminar I would be ready to meet the chela. I counted on his attendance as a given fact—all the area ECKists planned to attend.

Strangely, the voice of the Inner Master was silent now. I felt alone, adrift without a guide. The Inner Master had no more words for me.

The seminar day arrived. My eyes scanned the crowd. I sought the familiar face of the chela, ready and eager to fulfill my promise. But the seminar passed without him.

Maybe he had been called out of town or caught a bad cold, I reasoned inwardly. The desire to fulfill my promise grew insistently stronger.

I spoke to a friend about the seminar the next day. Casually, I asked if she had seen the chela. "Oh, Coleen." As she spoke, a funny look crossed her face. "Didn't you know? He translated (died) nearly two weeks ago."

Anguish and regret welled up within me, and two tears trickled down one cheek. I felt awkward and heavy—out of place. I had missed the opportunity to meet a new, old friend. But moreover, I'd broken my promise to the Inner Master through neglect. This last realization hit me like a punch in the nose, and my face reddened.

"I heard but didn't listen," I cried inwardly. From that moment on, I vowed to turn to the Inner Master daily for guidance and to live in the moment. The words, "Trust your inner knowingness, live in the moment, and listen to the Inner Master," rang through my daily contemplations.

As I accepted the spiritual challenge, I felt my life imperceptibly speed up. Instinctively, I knew I was on a fast track to somewhere.

A week and a half later, it was my turn to open the ECK Center. A fellow ECKist was moderating a class that evening. I found myself strangely attracted to him in an inexplicably neutral way. Shortly thereafter, my vow to the ECK was tested. "Call him up and ask him out," I heard, "—but not yet." Moment by moment, I checked with the Inner Master as days passed. One afternoon, I felt a shift. "Now . . . call him *now!*"

Chanting HU inwardly, I found my attitude to be surprisingly neutral. This person was someone I'd like to know as a friend, nothing more or less. And if the ECK felt it a part of my journey to know this individual, then I was not one to argue.

The phone clicked, and his groggy voice traveled through the line, "Hello?"

"I'm sorry, did I wake you?" Amid apologies, I did manage to stammer out who I was and an invitation to get together. Immediately my ego wanted to take it back and crawl into a hole. But Soul reigned, and a silence fell between us that couldn't have lasted even a minute, but felt like ten.

"Uh, yeah, sure, I guess so," he agreed. I wondered, had he checked on the inner, too? I laughed inwardly, and in that moment I found the freedom to be myself. As time passed, we got to know each other better.

About six weeks later, during a quiet time together, I wondered what it would be like to be married to this guy. The next words out of his mouth were, "Will you marry me?" Instantly I asked the Inner Master, "What do I say?" and the Inner Master replied, "Say yes!"

I never imagined that the way to love could be found by listening to the Inner Master, being true to myself, and living in the moment. But the Mahanta may use any experience along the journey to unfold the chela. This turned out to be a love story, but more than that. It also turned out to be the never-ending story of the most important relationship of all—the one between the chela and the Inner Master.

Into the Valley of Kings

Tonya Hancherow

In 1989, at the age of nineteen, I stood in the Valley of the Kings in Egypt. The searing midday sun left me feeling exhausted, so I headed up a hill to escape the heat and the peddlers clamoring to sell their wares. Halfway up the hill I entered the tomb of Ramses II. The crowds of tourists were too lazy to make the climb, and the chamber was empty except for one small Egyptian man, who sat on his haunches, leaning against the tunnel wall and slowly eating a tomato.

It struck me as odd that he did not ask for money as most of the natives did but simply studied me quietly as I walked by. There was an air of humility about him as though he too was in awe of his ancestors' work.

I walked on and entered a dim chamber. Suddenly I felt chilled and turned quickly to leave, but instead I found myself looking at the picture engraved upon the wall before me. It was a picture of a pharaoh extending his hand to the sun god, Ra. Tears welled up from within me as I realized that I was gazing at a picture which I myself had created many centuries ago.

Swept into the picture, I was catapulted back into

my life then as an artist whose deepest desire was to create work which would express the love within him. Yet he was a slave commanded by the pharaoh to create images on walls deep below the ground while a guard stood over him threatening his very existence.

In his dreams, the artist had seen visions brighter than Ra's wings. That is what he wished to paint. But he was of the lower class, and his wishes would never be heard, let alone considered. He was forced to create images that might have been painted with love—but instead hatred and contempt were in his heart.

I stood shaken and amazed by this experience. Tears streamed down my cheeks as I went forward and touched the wall. I heard the HU and felt it envelop me, releasing an incredible creative and spiritual frustration which was a holdover from the past.

My fingers ran over the grooved hieroglyphics as the ECK healed this three-thousand-year-old wound. I sang the HU and felt the healing love flow through me.

After doing a contemplation, I gathered myself up and prepared to return to the outside world. I turned toward the light and saw the man still leaning against the wall. His quiet presence seemed to be a confirmation of the Mahanta's blessing, and I thanked him as I walked past. He nodded in return, and I walked out into the sunlight.

For a Child Returned

Laurie Reams

When I went into labor on February 11, 1980, my husband and I had already arranged with the doctor not to have any unnecessary conversation or bright lights in the delivery room. After the baby was born, the staff would leave us alone for a minute with our new child.

So after seven pushes, Paul Matthew Reams was born at 8:55 p.m. He was cleaned up and brought back to me, and my husband, Jonathan, and I each held one of Paul's little hands and did a short HU Chant. We explained that he was in a physical body and we were his earthly parents for this incarnation. He relaxed once he knew what was going on.

As the months speedily passed, Paul grew into a chubby, smiling baby. He didn't have much hair yet, just a golden fuzziness—but bright blue knowing eyes. He went to many ECK functions with us and seemed to enjoy them.

One day in October, he seemed unusually sad and fretful. I put him down for his midmorning nap with an audiocassette of "Paulji Talks to the Children" to help settle him down a bit, while I read the beautiful poetry of Omar Khayyam's *Rubiyat*. Suddenly I realized the time had flown; it was nearly noon. I jumped up to make Jonathan's lunch.

Paul certainly was sleeping a long time. He hadn't napped this long (about two hours) in quite awhile. I checked to see if he was awake yet. He seemed sound asleep, but as I bent over the crib, his color seemed peculiar. I touched him—he wasn't breathing or moving at all. Gently I shook his shoulder and then lifted him up. He was all slack and rubbery in my arms.

I laid him on the floor and quickly started mouth-to-mouth resuscitation. I was alone in the apartment, working frantically over my baby, my heart beating so loud I couldn't hear myself think. Suddenly a warm, strong hand squeezed my shoulder and said, "Let him go." Gently I looked up—it was Rebazar Tarzs, the great ECK Master, with my son in his other arm. The beautiful smiles on their faces took away all my fear and anxiety. Then I realized others were standing there, too. Paul Twitchell and a shy-looking, slim man, wearing dark-rimmed glasses, whom I would later recognize as Sri Harold Klemp. There was a soft golden glow around them.

I called my husband, and we rushed to the hospital, but, of course, it was too late. I already knew my son was happiest where he was now.

As the months went by, I continued to see my son in my dreams. He was developing at about the same rate as he would have on the physical plane. I watched him progress from a chubby, crawling baby to a laughing toddler.

Then, during one visit in the summer of 1982, I noticed Paul was getting younger and smaller. I couldn't understand it. I asked the Inner Master why, but no answer came. Paul just kept getting younger and younger. By fall he was back to being a newborn. Then his appearance began changing to that of a baby girl with black wavy hair.

When the pregnancy test came back positive in October (the same date that Paul had translated, two years before), I really began to wonder. I didn't wonder any longer when at 6:00 a.m. on May 29, 1983, I gave birth to a black-haired baby girl named Melissa Karen.

The ECK sometimes works in mysterious ways, but eventually all is made clear.

A Debt Repaid—Fifty Years Later

Geri Shanafelt

As with many important events in my life, working with the hospice program started as a coincidence.

My husband and I just happened to stop by a friend's house one Sunday afternoon. As we visited, she told me she was very involved in organizing a new hospice group in a neighboring county. She said that hospices are run by people who believe that the individual has as much right to die as to live. They help the terminally ill patient who would rather die at home than in an impersonal hospital. I liked the philosophy.

Help is always needed in the home, she said. The hospice worker is on hand to lend a sympathetic ear, run errands, or give family members a break so they can leave the house for a while.

I decided then and there to volunteer my time and was immediately assigned to a woman in her seventies dying of lung cancer. Generally, the first meeting between hospice worker and patient occurs in the home. But I remembered meeting this lady once before, when we had both adopted a puppy from the same litter. It was something to talk about in the beginning.

After a few hours she opened up a little and started telling me about her illness. The lung cancer wasn't a surprise. "When I had heart trouble," she said, "the doctor told me to stop smoking. Then I had leg problems, and the doctor again said, 'Stop smoking!' This time, when I couldn't breathe, I knew. I guess after three strikes, you're out."

I left her home with a special feeling of warmth and love that I could not explain. That night I had an interesting dream experience. The year was 1937. I was waiting, as Soul, for a physical body, but the woman aborted the pregnancy. When I awoke, I realized that the woman was my hospice patient. It had taken almost fifty years for me to meet her in the physical world.

The next day she confided (for whatever private reasons) that she had had an abortion in 1937. It was as close as she ever came to having a child. The materials for a baby quilt, which she had started to embroider all those years ago, had been neatly packed away in a suitcase. I was working on a quilt at the time, and this had sparked the conversation.

Suddenly she rose from her bed and pulled out a stack of beautifully stitched pieces of yellow cloth. "I don't know why, but I want you to have these," she said. At that moment I knew that whatever karma had existed between us was now dissolved. Only love remained, from one Soul to another.

She died several weeks later. As a hospice volunteer, the relationships I have with patients are not always so clear, but I am grateful for the chance to share the love I receive each day during my ECK Spiritual Exercises, and hospice is a good way for me to learn more about detachment, divine love, and the 360-degree overview of Soul.

Pop's Reincarnation

Dee Meredith

As an ECKist, I often wondered how to prove reincarnation to myself. Were my flashbacks from previous lives just imagination?

About fifteen months ago, my father translated (died). I didn't attend his burial service, but I was honored to be present inwardly as he awoke in the Astral world. Before long he was up and about, learning about his new home in the inner worlds.

Ever so often I would stop in during my spiritual contemplations to see how he was doing. I was amused to find that the spiritual principles we discussed before his death were becoming a reality for him now.

These visits went on for about ten months. Then one day, I stopped by to chat with Pop, and he wasn't there. At first I thought he'd just gone off exploring and would return. But when I asked the Inner Master, I was told he was preparing for another incarnation on the earth plane. I was surprised, but I realized that as Soul, Pop must continue on.

One day at work, I heard a soft voice inside my head telling me to watch for my father's incarnation in a few months. I wondered about this, especially since I couldn't think of any woman I knew who was pregnant.

Then I remembered meeting a young couple just after my dad translated. We had immediately become fast friends; I felt I had known them for years. She was pregnant now, and I had a knowingness that Dad would return as her baby.

I went to visit my friend the day she came home from the hospital. Everyone was crowded around the baby when I got there. When I got my first glimpse of the newborn, I immediately noticed his physical structure was like my dad's old body. He had the same unmanageable fine hair and the yellowish complexion that ran in our blood line.

Silently, I welcomed this Soul back as I picked the baby up. With intent alertness, his little untrained eyes tried to focus on me. As I touched his Third Eye with my forefinger, a golden light radiated outward and engulfed his entire head. His three-day-old baby face twisted into a lopsided grin of recognition.

I could feel him straining to move his vocal cords. With great effort, he screamed out my nickname! His new parents were speechless. A ripple of love spread through the room, and we all began to laugh.

In that moment, a wealth of information was shared between me and the baby. I can only describe it as an instant swapping of information, Soul to Soul. One thing I sensed was that Dad felt really scrunched up in that tiny body!

I keep track of this Soul through his parents, dropping by for a visit every so often. When he hears my voice, there's always a familiar lopsided grin on his face to welcome me.

A Guiltless New Life in ECK

Donna Russ

Late on the night of December 7, my three-year-old son and I travel the icy roads of southern Georgia. Randy is lying sweetly on the backseat when we come to the curved bridge.

He is fast asleep when the car spins out of control and flips over, crashing through the guardrail and landing upside down in the backwater of the river.

Trapped in the front seat I grope, panic-stricken, for my sleeping son. (The crash has thrown his small body through the rear window. He is already dead.)

Water rushes into the car, icy cold, taking away what breath I have. I keep gulping for air and swallowing only water as I struggle to find a way to reach my son and then get out of the car.

Soon I realize I am going to die; thoughts race to my family, and I hope they will be all right.

My body feels like it's turning somersaults over and over. Completely out of air, I scream in my mind, "God, help me!"

A brilliant flash of white light fills my vision. I feel the pressure of gentle hands grasping my wrists, pulling me upward in a sort of wavy motion.

I am standing next to the car, waist-deep in icy water. No one is around, and I feel confused. I gasp out, "Who pulled me from the upside-down wreck?" Shock and numbness settle softly around me, and I don't remember much of those next few days—the events of twenty years ago.

The night after my son's funeral, I remember asking, "Why can't Randy be brought back to life like Jesus was?" Instantly, I heard angels singing.

But was Randy in heaven? My husband's church believed in baptism at age ten or twelve. I had followed his wishes in not baptizing our baby at birth, even though my Lutheran upbringing demanded it.

The next day, the Lutheran minister came to our house and told me I had condemned my child to hell. So for the next fifteen years I prayed but one prayer: "Please take Randy into heaven, God. He was a sweet, innocent baby, and it was due to my neglect that he wasn't baptized."

Many times I wondered why I had been spared; was it just to suffer the guilt of his death? I had been blessed with five more children since the accident, but somehow Randy's presence still seemed so near.

Then five years ago I was introduced to Eckankar. I learned to work with the spiritual exercises and discovered the truth about life after death, the truth about my son.

Since Randy had shown signs of being slightly retarded, I truly believe he chose to translate to another world. This was so that he, as Soul, could come back in a more perfect body.

There was no actual insight other than a feeling and a look in the eyes, but I began to know that my daughter, Pam, was very special. Perhaps she came to me in Randy's stead—or perhaps Randy chose to visit our family again.

It felt so good to have an inkling of the truth. The guilt was being replaced by knowledge.

I have found great peace in my life. Through Eckankar, I've also learned many things that church never taught me. There truly is life after death; reincarnation is true! As an initiate of Eckankar, with the help of the Inner Master, I also learned that I don't have to come back to this earth for countless incarnations.

I am on my way up the path I sought for so long. Randy is still close to my heart—and so is the Inner Master!

2
There Is No Death

Life goes on and on and on...

Across the Veil

Bob Lawton

Most people think that no one knows, or can know, what lies beyond death. Is it our religious upbringing that makes us believe that death flings the Soul upon some far mystical shore, from which no traveler ever returns?

I'm a professional fire fighter. One night after a busy fourteen-hour shift, I returned home exhausted. I didn't waste a moment snuggling into bed for a well-earned rest.

But even dead tired, I rolled onto my back and closed my eyes for a short spiritual exercise. I had gotten into the habit of doing this contemplation to prepare for sleep. A spiritual exercise attunes the physical self with Spirit. It also helps you accept and remember your dream journeys.

As I drift off, I hear a voice calling my name. I place my attention on it and try to recognize the familiar tone. I know that voice and start moving toward it. As I get closer, I sense fear and questioning.

Oh, I know. It's Dad. As soon as I thought the word *Dad,* there he was, standing in front of me with a puzzled look on his face.

"Dad, what's the matter?"

"I'm not sure. I'm...I was...ah, I guess it's this strange dream...not knowing where I am or knowing how to get back. Then I knew you were out there, so I called out to you. Bob, can I be dreaming and know it at the same time?"

"Dad, sometimes it takes a dream to lead us to where we need to go. Like now. I guess you're on a journey, maybe toward the place that I was headed for, and you felt me pass through this plane.

"There are many planes of reality—what people call heaven—but in Eckankar, with the help of the Mahanta, the Living ECK Master, we're able to get to the highest planes. He guides us through these lower ones, keeping us from getting lost or drifting into the vastness, out of control."

"But why? Why do we come here?"

"Well, you know how you get that inner yearning to return home after you've been away for a long time? It's like that. As Soul we yearn to return to our true world, and as we get closer, there's an overwhelming love that surrounds us. That's the divine love of God one encounters on his journey homeward through the higher planes.

"The Living ECK Master takes us on these inner journeys to link us up with the Light and Sound. Dad, would you like to meet him?"

"Yes, Bob, I think so."

My dad took one step forward. As he did, the color of the plane began to change to different shades. Simultaneously we seemed to be flung upward very fast. A buzzing vibration entered me and there was a tingling sensation. My father smiled.

"You feel that?" I asked.

He nodded, not saying anything as if not wanting to disturb the moment. I looked and saw a bluish-golden glow off to his left.

"Dad, this is the Living ECK Master," I said as I watched the bluish-glowing bubble pulse, stabilize, and form into the appearance of the Outer Master, Sri Harold Klemp.

Dad turned his head, smiled, and said, "Oh, I've seen you before. I think I know you, don't I?"

* * *

Returning from the inner spiritual experience, I opened my eyes with no feeling or thought of sleepiness. Quickly I searched my thoughts, as if looking for an appropriate arrangement of words—words that I knew would never be able to describe what had taken place.

I bolted upright and jumped from the bed all in one movement. Hopping into my pants, I quickly yelled downstairs to my wife, "Get ready, we're going to see my father!" He had just been admitted to the hospital the day before.

We raced over there. When the elevator opened at Dad's floor, my attention was immediately drawn to a man a few steps ahead, walking down the hall. Even though I had never laid eyes on him before, I knew this man was my father's doctor.

As we rounded the corner to enter the same room, he turned and asked who I was there to see. When I told him, he replied, "Oh, I'm so sorry! Your father just passed away. They called me just a minute ago. I have to confirm it legally for the death certificate."

"I know," I said.

With a funny look on his face, he asked, "You know? But no one has been notified!"

"That's OK. I think I'll go in now."

I walked into the room and slipped past the curtain they had drawn. I stood at the side of the bed, saying my silent farewell.

"I bless you in the name of the Mahanta, the Living ECK Master. You're in the best of hands."

A warmth came from within. My dad had passed on. This was only his lifeless shell. Yet we had walked that journey together—a journey not shared by many, where one stays behind. I thanked Spirit— the ECK—and the Living ECK Master for allowing me to help my father cross through the veil.

What I had read in the teachings of Eckankar was true: We can help someone who has died across the borders of death and put him in the hands of friends.

Does Part of Us Live On?

Jackie Christian

The phone rang. It was my sister in Kentucky. Her husband, Gene, was scheduled for immediate surgery. Could I come stay with her? Gene had noticed a mole on his right shoulder getting larger and darker, and he felt intuitively it might be serious. I flew up to be with them during and after the surgery.

The mole was diagnosed as a melanoma—a malignant tumor. The surgeon performed aggressive surgery on the area around the mole, also removing the lymph nodes under the arm as a preventive measure. As further insurance, my brother-in-law would travel monthly to a nearby university hospital for regular chemotherapy treatments.

I returned home, but my sister and I communicated weekly. We discussed this experience—the causes and effects, the changes in all of us, the fears and anxieties we were facing—asking questions, seeking answers.

As a student of Eckankar, I was learning to look for the spiritual lessons and principles behind each experience. My sister was aware of my beliefs and was very open to them. She often initiated conversations about her own spiritual search for understanding in this difficult situation. I shared a simple spiritual exercise with her: sing the ancient name for God, HU, in times of need, for guidance and upliftment from the Holy Spirit.

During that first year, my sister was unable to consider the possibility that her husband might die. They pursued every avenue to combat this attack upon his system.

The chemotherapy made my brother-in-law very ill. For days following a treatment, he would be unable to go to work. Then he would be all right for a few weeks until his next treatment. This routine continued throughout the next year. It had its effect on the body, but his spirit soared. The illness had a transforming effect upon him.

Gene was a deeply caring person, but before his illness, he was often unable to express his feelings. This changed. Now he seemed to savor the fullness of each moment. Love seemed to pour out of him, embracing those who were part of that moment.

After twelve months of chemotherapy, my brother-in-law was given a clean bill of health. This seemed especially wonderful since he was the only one in his treatment group to survive the first year. He returned to work with a grateful heart.

Toward the end of the second year, however, he began to have digestive problems. His doctor scheduled him for exploratory surgery, and again we all went to the hospital. Cancer had spread to all his organs. There was no hope.

My brother-in-law deteriorated rapidly from that point on. Only occasionally was he able to return to work. My sister, a schoolteacher, wanted to take a leave of absence to stay home with him. But he asked her to continue with her life.

Theirs was a special relationship. Yet my sister was very dependent on him emotionally. She had counted on him to be there at least until their youngest child, who was in junior high, was raised. Now she had to face his impending death.

With the help of a hospice program, Gene was able to remain at home. One of my sister's fears was that he would die while she was at work. Every evening she rushed back home, afraid that he would be gone.

My sister and I remained in constant contact. She told me that she and her husband were trying to make every moment count. They discussed finances; she noted his advice carefully. He asked for a celebration service in their church sanctuary instead of a funeral, and he arranged for his body to be cremated so my sister wouldn't be tied to a plot of ground where his body was buried. He did everything he could to make his passing easier. Such was his love for her.

I asked the ECK and my sister what help I could give during these trying times. My brother-in-law was a sincerely religious person and did not struggle against death. But his acceptance and readiness was incomprehensible to my sister. She wanted him to fight, even though his body was beyond repair. Would he survive as Soul, even after death? she wondered. She wasn't sure. She had no proof. If she knew, she told me, it would make it so much easier.

Everything had been done that could be. The physician said there was no way his body could survive another week. Gene told my sister how very tired he was. She released her emotional hold on him—but something was still keeping him from dying. One day she called to ask for my opinion. "Why can't he go?"

As we talked, I inwardly chanted the sacred name for God, HU, to open my heart to the Holy Spirit.

Suddenly I asked her if anyone was praying for him to be healed. She said surely not; everyone understood they didn't want to interfere with God's wishes. But she decided to check into it.

Later that day she called and told me that the religious group her oldest daughter belonged to—who believed in faith healing—was praying for him. They were ignorant of the laws of Spirit and didn't know they were holding him here in the physical world! She thanked them for their love and concern, but asked that they stop their specific prayer and simply release him to the Holy Spirit, to allow Its will to be done. She made it clear that his fate was between him and God.

Gene died, or translated to another plane of existence, shortly thereafter. It was a Sunday morning, and my sister was with him, as she had wanted—just the two of them. Immediately I flew to be with her and help with the final details.

It's strange, but now I can't remember what day it was—whether before or after his celebration service. But one morning I woke up and heard my brother-in-law singing.

It was his favorite song, which we all loved. He had a marvelous voice and often sang this melody at family gatherings. I was so excited. I turned to see if my sister was awake. She was. I told her I heard Gene singing!

Her face lit up. Then with a look of bewilderment and disbelief, she exclaimed that she heard him singing too. Quickly, she asked me what song I heard him singing. I told her. Yes—it was the same one she heard!

My sister had asked for proof that Soul, our essence, continued after death. She had wondered if her husband was happy. Now the ECK had given her just the experience she needed so she would no longer wonder. She knew!

There Is No Death

Ann Archer Butcher

Ten years ago, I was teaching high school during
the day and working on my master's degree at
night. One night as I prepared to leave for my evening
classes, my head began to hurt. A feeling came over me
that someone close to me was dying. I was alarmed. I
immediately turned to a friend who was with me and
asked, "Jon, do you feel well?"

He felt fine, but I didn't. My head was hurting
terribly now, and the feeling of death was becoming
more intense. I called my mother long-distance. She
felt fine. I called my sister in New York. No answer, but
this was not unusual for her.

I sat down to try to relieve my headache. With my
eyes open, I clearly saw a black, cone-shaped tunnel of
great length—large at my end but receding rapidly to a
small pinpoint of light. I told Jon what I saw and then
blurted out with great distress, "I am going through the
tunnel!...It's so cold!...I'm going so fast!"

I was experiencing all this while sitting in my living
room with my eyes wide open! Almost shouting now, I

told my friend, "There's a light, a bright light at the end. I'm going through it!"

My teeth were chattering, and I was freezing cold. Suddenly, I hit the light. It was so intense that I became extremely hot and felt nearly blinded. Then I received an inner message. It ran through my head like a line of ticker tape. I was told emphatically to close my eyes.

When I did, I could see better; my eyes no longer burned. I stepped forward and found I was neither hot nor cold. Although I was still sitting on my living room couch, I was also stepping consciously into a beautiful ocean unlike anything I had ever seen or imagined.

It was a gold-and-white sea of light, which undulated around me in big, sparkling waves. But the waves did not rush against my legs; they went right through me, flooding me with love and beauty and joy. I knew I could stand there forever.

But I was called upon to do more than simply soak up the glory of this amazing environment. Suddenly I began to receive more inner messages. I was told there were ten things I must remember.

But I was enjoying myself and felt no sense of urgency. I didn't really want to feel anything but this moment. I probably won't remember much, I thought to myself.

Quickly I was told I would remember everything. And then, one by one, I received the following list of ten instructions:

1. Although you have absolutely no intellectual knowledge of what is occurring here, someone very close to you *appears* to be dying.

2. In truth, there is no death—only the illusion of death.

3. However, upon learning of this apparent death, you must go at once to this person.

4. In order to help this person, you will be instructed and must follow these instructions.

5. You must tell everyone concerned: this is not death!

6. After this experience, this person will be better off than ever before...

7. ...but it will not appear to be so.

8. You must leave when you are told to do so, although you will not wish to...

9. ...for you have much to do. You must listen carefully and do as you are instructed.

10. Remember, everything is always happening exactly as it should, whether it appears that way or not.

Despite these clear instructions, when I felt urged to leave a few moments later I had no desire to go. As I looked from the waist-high waves in which I stood, I spied a huge fountain; it rose up as high as I could see. It appeared to be the magnificent source for the ocean in which I bathed. Its waters flowed out like liquid light in massive golden streams, sparkling and brilliant. A beautiful sound completely filled the air.

I was transfixed by the scene and struggled to stay just a bit longer. But suddenly I was sucked back through the tunnel, traveling at breakneck speed into its freezing, constricted depths.

The tunnel was as terrible as the ocean was magnificent. Then suddenly I was back on my couch. My friend Jon was still with me, staring in disbelief and asking what happened. I tried to tell him, but I felt like crying. I was still shivering from the cold tunnel.

I found my way to a mirror and looked at my face. My eyes were bloodshot—red and swollen, as though they had been sunburned by an intense light. Jon assured me I had never left the couch, but clearly *something* had happened.

As the terrible headache faded I decided to go to my evening class and perhaps forget the whole thing. But first I sat down and wrote out the instructions I had received—one through ten. I gave the paper to Jon and asked him to keep it for me. "It may be important later," I told him. Right now I wanted to get on with my life.

That night I struggled to pay attention in class. There was a guest instructor I especially wanted to hear. But he spoke for only a short time before faltering in his presentation. He stopped, looked at me directly, and then told the class to take a ten-minute break. He approached me even before I could get out of my seat. "Strange as it might seem," he said, "you appear to be glowing with a bright light all around you!"

I knew absolutely nothing about this sort of thing. It was certainly far more than my mind was prepared to deal with. I excused myself from class saying, "I don't feel well, actually." I left and went home to hide under my covers!

Although it was spring and the weather had been warm, I awoke the next morning to discover a light snow covering the ground. The sun was shining brightly on this white blanket, and the world seemed refreshingly clean and peaceful. I felt confident that no loved ones were actually dying and went happily off to work.

I was busy teaching when I was called down to the office. I found Jon waiting there. He turned and quickly told me, "It's your sister. You have to go to New York right away."

I was stunned. I asked how she was. He told me she appeared to be dying. (Obviously, he had read the notes from the night before!)

My sister Debbe was very close to death. Jon immediately rushed me to the airport, and I flew to join my mother in New York. As we rushed to Debbe's bedside, I assured Mom that my sister was not really dying.

When I saw Debbe she was as white as a ghost—surrounded by an oxygen tent, machines, and nurses. I went right in and felt I should touch her head. As soon as I did this, I felt the terrible headache return from the night before. Slowly, Debbe opened her eyes and spoke to me, saying she had a terrible headache. As she said a few words to my mother, I saw an image of a balloon in my sister's head—a deflated, burst balloon.

I told my mom, and we asked to see the surgeon right away. When he arrived, I somehow found the courage to tell him what I sensed. I asked if there could possibly be a balloon in Debbe's head.

To my surprise, he listened intently and said, "Yes, that could be an aneurysm—a stretched and weakened blood vessel or capillary which has ballooned out and burst."

I found myself telling him where the balloon was and what type it was. Then I thought to ask him why he was paying attention to what I said. He replied, "I've seen this before. In these circumstances, others sometimes know more than I. If the aneurysm is where you described it, I feel I can operate and your sister will live." We signed the papers for him to do the surgery.

Debbe was operated on, the aneurysm was discovered, and the surgery was successful. We were elated. Debbe was alive and well, talking to us, writing friends, and recovering nicely.

Days later, however, she suffered a stroke, and was paralyzed on one side. This was a devastating blow, but I remembered the words, "After this experience, this person will be better off than ever before … but it will not appear to be so."

Debbe endured a lengthy struggle to regain use of her left leg. As I stood by and watched, I saw her grow stronger in Spirit, and more thoughtful and concerned for others.

As the years went by, Debbe was confronted with many challenges. Although she was unable to conquer the paralysis completely, she returned to her accounting career and began her life again. She fell in love, remarried, and just two years ago had her second son.

Life has not been easy for her, but since the operation Debbe has surprised me again and again with her strength and courage. She has even come to my rescue when I needed her.

As I watch her blossom and grow, it seems that within this one lifetime Debbe has been given a chance to live two lives. I have come to realize that she *is* better than ever before, just as I was told she would be.

As for me, I found the path of Eckankar shortly after my sister's stroke. Through the Spiritual Exercises of ECK, I learned that my journey had been through the tunnel of death. I had bathed that night in the vast Ocean of Love and Mercy—the source of all life. I have since been able to revisit this sea and pierce the illusion of death. I am still awed by this experience—but I have discovered even greater wonders on this magnificent path of Eckankar!

Dad's Gift from the "Other Side"

Monica Wylie

I was about fifteen when my father died of a heart attack. He'd been born with a heart problem. Growing up, I sometimes felt I was the cause of my father's painful angina. He always wanted to do things with me, but my pace was too fast.

One day while I was at school, I had a sudden knowingness that my father was about to leave us. I saw him inwardly as he sat reading an Eckankar book. He said, "I want to rest."

Then in my inner vision he laid the book down in his lap and translated to another plane of reality. I sensed my family's concern reaching out to me at school, and I couldn't concentrate. When I got home later that day, everybody was peering out the window, waiting for me. My mom opened the door for me, and when I saw her standing there, I knew.

I took it badly because I missed my dad's physical presence. I missed him hugging me and holding me, his touch, and his voice. But because I had grown up with Spirit, the ECK, I wasn't angry. Inwardly, I knew this was simply a translation to a new life for him.

That night, though, I was afraid to go to bed by myself. I'd never been afraid like this before! I wanted to sleep with my mom, but she wanted to be alone. When I got in bed I felt my father's presence in my room, so I clutched the sheets up to my eyes, ready to cover my head.

Suddenly Dad appeared, walking toward my bed. He had his white sweater and his glasses on, as though he were physically there. As he walked toward the bed, I felt scared—though I sensed he didn't want to scare me. I felt Dad gently say, "Don't be scared, Monica."

My first reaction was to jump under the covers. As a child, I would sometimes see ghosts in my room, so covering my head with the blankets was an old habit. But after a moment, I pulled the sheet down. Dad was still standing there. I remember apologizing for being so scared, and Dad just said, "Don't be scared. You know better, now that you've been in ECK for so long."

Dad came closer. As he walked by my foot, he gave it an affectionate slap. "I love you," he said. I felt his strong fingers hit my foot, just like he'd always do in the morning to wake me up. Then the vision faded. This was Dad's signal that he was off to say good-bye to a few other people.

My experience was verified by a friend of my father's, who had felt a slap on his back. He turned around saying, "What the heck was that?" and saw my father. Dad used these familiar touches to let people know he was all right.

I dreamed about Dad, too. One night he came to take me dancing with him. I said, "No, Dad, I would rather watch." As I looked on, he danced with several nondescript beings. I felt his joy at being able to dance, finally free from the pain of angina.

As time went on, we watched each other grow. It wasn't important to my father how I grew up physically, only how I grew spiritually. Dad would drive up in his blue car during a dream or spiritual exercise, and we would visit different heavenly planes. He'd take me to see this scene or that sight in the inner worlds—or sometimes to a park, where the Inner Master, the Mahanta, would teach us from my father's ECK discourses. We progressed through the Astral and Mental planes. Now I visit him on the Etheric Plane. He doesn't have glasses anymore, and he appears thinner and much finer. That's the real him. You see, as he gets higher, I see him more as pure Soul.

One day he said, "I'm not your father anymore—remember that. I only worked as your father on the physical plane. But always remember, the love of being your father is still there. I love you, and you love me, and that's how it is now." I can't wait to pass this love on to my children.

I keep learning from this Soul, a gift for which I'm very grateful to the Inner Master. The man who was my father is a Co-worker with God now—that's his true occupation. He's in the inner worlds, though he's also still in my heart. And someday, I'll be a Co-worker with God just like him.

Becoming a Co-worker with God

Virginia Siekerka

Mom always said I asked more questions than the rest of the kids. Even after Mom died, I continued to ask her questions.

Sometimes she would appear in my dreams. Other times I would wake up in the middle of the night and find her lying next to me in bed. Startled, I would ask, "Mom, what are you doing here? You're dead!"

She would reply, "Oh no, I'm not dead. I'm very much alive." I would feel her presence off and on during the day. Because of my ever-burning curiosity, I'd question her: "Mom, what are you doing, where you are?"

She'd say, "I'm helping people on the earth plane get rid of their fears." When I queried her further, she'd say, "I'm not supposed to answer any more questions now—got to go! I love you!"

After a period of years, I was told through an inner voice that Mom had gone into "progression"; I would not be hearing from her again. I readily accepted this inner wisdom, because to me, the word *progression* implied that Mom had done her job well and learned what she needed to learn. Now she was moving on to another level. So with understanding and a loving heart, I silently wished Mom well. I was happy for her, but somehow I knew that one day I would hear from her again.

Many years later, as a young woman living in Chicago, I took a secretarial job at a chemical research company. Seven secretaries and five researchers with doctorates were housed in a small office on the second floor of an old walk-up building.

One of the women working in this office was just seventeen years old. Our shared sense of humor made for an immediate friendship—or so it seemed on the surface.

One day on a coffee break, she said she'd known me before. I was aware she was referring to prior lifetimes, but I pretended I knew nothing of such things. It was an interesting topic for me, but this was the 1950s— long before I found Eckankar. I had learned not to voice my inner knowingness.

I asked my new friend what she meant, and she replied, "When I was eight years old I had a dream. You were in that dream with four other people. The five of you are very important to me, and I will meet all of you in this lifetime."

She said I was the first person in the dream that she had met—and that I would help her spiritually. She asked me many questions about myself and told me of her inner experiences in past lives and in this life. We would often chat the lunch hour away.

I learned that she was married to a young fellow who was an alcoholic. In his drunken state he abused her. Often she slept in the bathroom with the door locked, afraid that he might kill her.

One night as she was huddled on the bathroom floor, something gently touched her shoulder. A beautiful lady appeared, and her fear vanished. She slept the rest of the night in peace on the floor. This went on for weeks. Every morning at work, my friend would tell me, "The beautiful lady appeared again last night."

One morning I asked her, "This lady who comes to see you—who is she?"

"I don't know," she said.

"Well, why don't you ask her?" I suggested.

A few mornings later, my friend seated herself at her desk and immediately turned to me, saying, "I know the lady's name—she told me." And she pronounced the name clearly and carefully: "Pearl Barbara Kascza."

I sat speechless at my desk, feeling completely overwhelmed by this news. Apparently I looked strange, because my friend urged me to come into the ladies' lounge. I followed her numbly, and she seated me on the couch. Finally, feeling as though I was returning from an out-of-body experience, I said, "Why do you keep asking me if I'm all right?"

Gently taking my arm, she lifted me from the couch and stood me in front of the mirror. "Look!"

For a second I didn't recognize myself. My face was drained of color, as if I'd forgotten to apply my make-up that morning. "I have something to tell you," I said, turning to my friend.

"This lady who has been appearing to you is my mother," I told her. "You've given her first name, her middle name, and her maiden name."

My friend had never heard me refer to my mother in any way but as "Mom." Back in those days, in that generation, we did not refer to our parents by their first names.

I remembered Mom had told me she helped people here on earth with their fears. What a confirmation! My heart was filled with love and comfort. This outer experience paved the way for my later discovery of Eckankar. I knew its teachings were true: that, as Soul, we are immortal—and our goal in this lifetime is to become loving Co-workers with God.

The Death (and Rebirth) of a Young ECKist

Dee Taylor

It's been a year since my sixteen-year-old daughter, Anna Dee, translated (died) in an automobile accident. She had been on the path of Eckankar most of her life.

I was in Mexico on a skin-diving trip at the time, and my other daughter, Shannon, was out surfing. Anna Dee had just gotten her driver's license thirteen days earlier. Before I left home, I told Anna where to find the keys to the car and asked her not to go out of town.

Shannon said the whole week I was gone, Anna Dee seemed different. She was very excited and filled with love. The day she translated, I was diving in the reefs of a beautiful bay. My right eye started to tear. I couldn't stop the rivulet which flowed down my cheek. I kept saying to myself, Go call home.

I called home that evening, and my son said, "Mom, hurry home, Anna Dee's dead." She had taken her friends for a drive. They weren't hurt but she had left her body instantly. My first instinct was to start the

67

nineteen-hour drive home immediately. But an inner voice said, "No, don't go yet. There are cows in the road." This was Mexico. So I waited.

I went to my camper and did a spiritual contemplation. After a short period of waiting, I saw Anna Dee. She was in the inner worlds, surrounded by several of the ECK Masters, including Wah Z. Wah Z is the spiritual name of the Living ECK Master, Sri Harold Klemp.

I said, "Anna Dee, do you know that you've translated?"

"Yes," she replied. "But I'm worried about my friends."

I turned to Wah Z for reassurance. "Well," I said to Anna Dee, "Why don't you fill yourself with a lot of love. It will help settle your thoughts."

She started generating this huge glowing ball of light. As I sat in contemplation the wind rose in the trees. Over the hills the dogs started barking intensely. Her love, like the ball of light, became stronger and stronger.

All of a sudden, this globe of light shot like a comet across my inner vision. My business partner, who was sitting on the other side of my camper, called out, "What was that flash of light?" Stunned, I said, "That was Anna Dee leaving the lower worlds."

When I got home, there was a lot of negative energy around the house. It was fear, generated by friends and family members unfamiliar with death.

I chanted HU for a few minutes, then I lay down to do another spiritual exercise. In contemplation, I saw Anna Dee being reborn in the inner worlds. I saw her as a little eagle! Slowly she was working her way out of a shell and into a new life. The next day, my daughter

Shannon came home and shared a similar inner experience. She saw Anna Dee being born into another world, on a far-distant planet.

I saw Anna Dee on and off in my contemplation periods over the next weeks. One day I asked her, "Were you frightened during the accident?"

"No," she said. "I just went into the light. In that split second, only my Physical and Astral bodies were driving the car. I was already in the higher worlds. There was no pain, Mom." She told me she might return to the earth plane, but wouldn't know for sure until about five months had passed. As I looked at my calendar later, I realized that would be around the time of the World Wide of ECK seminar.

Five months later, I went to the seminar—a large, three-day spiritual gathering of ECKists and interested seekers. I attended workshops, roundtable forums, and talks on Spirit. Was Anna Dee coming back, I wondered? I knew I'd find my answer soon.

On Saturday evening, Sri Harold Klemp spoke from the main stage. During his talk, I suddenly left my body. I saw Wah Z standing with Anna Dee. They walked up to me, and Wah Z put her hand in mine. I said, "Anna Dee, do you know if you're coming back?"

Anna Dee said, "I don't know."

"Well," I comforted her, "I don't know either, but the Master sees a lot more than we can." Then the experience ended.

The next morning, about an hour before Sri Harold's final talk of the seminar, I did a contemplation. All of sudden I had my answer. Somehow I knew Anna Dee was coming back—probably in my lifetime. It could be that I will know her, perhaps as a grandchild.

Sri Harold spoke that morning about the many Souls who will be coming to earth straight from the higher worlds. They will help point the way back to God in the times ahead. It was the Master's way of showing me on the inner and outer planes that Soul continues in Its mission to serve God by helping others.

It was my gift from Wah Z.

I Won't Walk Alone When I Die

Loretta Mirakhor

A t 1:00 a.m., Sunday morning, the howling and barking of the neighbor's dogs woke me. My son and I were visiting with my parents in Colorado for a week after a camping trip. I went to the upstairs window and groggily peered out. Maybe a stray cat or skunk was roaming the neighborhood.

Suddenly a feeling of apprehension crept up my spine. Not wanting to disturb the household, I quietly searched the house. Nothing wrong downstairs; Mom and Dad were sleeping peacefully. Why wouldn't this awful feeling go away?

I became aware of a presence in the kitchen. I felt no danger, just a spine-chilling impression of someone crying desperately for help. A few minutes passed, and then the presence was gone.

Reflecting on the past few minutes, I wondered if I was going to follow in my aunt's footsteps. She was often able to see and communicate with ghosts. A chill swept over me, and I said aloud, "I hope this is an isolated incident!"

I climbed back into bed and reached for my copy of *Dialogues with the Master* by Paul Twitchell. My oldest son had given me several books about Eckankar to read on my trip. It seemed to have the answers I was seeking.

Thoughts of the ECK and Sri Harold Klemp, the Living ECK Master, drifted through my head as I fell back to sleep. Again, the howling and barking of dogs woke me. This time the presence was in my room. A cold sweat drenched me. Who was coming to me for help? What could I do? The presence faded as suddenly as it had come, and the dogs stopped barking, but sleep was a long time coming.

The next morning, my younger sister and her husband came to tell us that tragedy had struck. My older sister's son had been hit by a tow truck while crossing a street in Chicago. He was in a coma, lingering between life and death.

After the initial shock wore off, I realized that the presence seeking my help might be my nephew who was being kept alive by machines. I knew I had to do something, but what? I certainly couldn't discuss my experience with the family. I asked the Living ECK Master to help my nephew find peace. It seemed so natural to do this, even though I really hadn't made any decisions about Eckankar. That night, the life-support machines were turned off, and my nephew died.

He came to see me again though, on Monday evening. He was still pleading for help and didn't understand what had happened to him. "I don't know how to help you. If you will only seek the Living ECK Master, I'm sure he will be able to help."

The impression came back that he didn't understand what I was trying to tell him. I repeated again that there was only one way I knew to get help. "Ask the Living ECK Master to guide you. Please do this one thing, and ask for Wah Z—that's the spiritual name of the Living ECK Master. He will help."

My nephew left. I was not certain that I had advised him to do the right thing, for I only had my feelings to go by. But the next evening, my nephew visited me for the last time. At first I thought he still needed help, then it struck me he was not alone. Somebody was with him, and they were both bathed in a glowing light. I felt a cascade of love and peace. My nephew spoke. "I came to say good-bye. I wanted you to know I found the Living ECK Master. I'm not afraid anymore. I'm not alone."

I felt somebody kiss me on the cheek, and then I received a big hug. "Thank you, Aunt Loretta, I love you." He was gone.

Back home, I reflected on the gift my nephew had bestowed. In his last visit to me, with the Living ECK Master, he had helped me remove my fear of death. Needless to say, I am now a student of Eckankar. I know I won't walk alone when I leave this physical world.

And He Had the Sweetest Smile

Ann Reddock

There was always a gap in communication between myself and my father, a practical, well-grounded inventor. Though a creative genius, Dad never allowed his subjective experiences to interfere with logic. He never quite understood how I looked at life until April of 1982. It was then that I also had the opportunity to truly know my father as Soul.

He became ill in March of that year and was scheduled for a series of operations. Since he lived alone, I moved in with Dad after his second operation. For the first time in his life, he was afraid of being alone—afraid that he might die.

I knew that, as Soul, we never really die. Death is simply a transition to another state of consciousness. However, I wanted to help my father prepare for the next step. Inwardly, I asked the Mahanta, the Inner Master, for guidance.

One night, Dad almost did die. Fortunately, Ron, who is now my husband, was with us, and he knew CPR. We were able to revive Dad and rush him to the

75

hospital. When I visited him, Soul was vacillating between the Physical body and Astral body.

As I stood next to his bed, he pointed at the television in his hospital room: "Oh, look! All my friends are up there." He began to call off their names, not realizing that the television wasn't on. I waited a minute, then reached over and gently touched his arm. "Who was *that*, Daddy?" I prompted.

When I touched him, he returned to the physical consciousness. As we talked about this astral experience, I realized the Mahanta was offering my father a simple example of other realms of life. In the five days that followed, miracles began to happen, sometimes hour by hour.

One day as he sat in bed with his eyes closed, he suddenly held up his hands, as if he were reading the paper. He turned the pages, and as he "read," he began to chuckle. I reached over and touched his arm. "Daddy? What are you doing?"

He said, "Well, Honey, can't you see? I'm reading the Sunday paper." I gave his arm a little squeeze, and it brought him back to his physical body. "What were you doing, Daddy?" I asked again.

"Well, I was reading the Sunday paper," he said quizzically, "but it's not here." I explained that he certainly *was* reading the paper—in another body that he would occupy soon. He was simply practicing how to use this new body.

Another time, he sat in bed with his eyes wide open, holding an invisible bowl, feeding himself. I reached over and stopped him, asking, "What are you doing, Daddy?"

"Well, Honey, obviously I'm eating my oatmeal," he said, a bit piqued. I squeezed a little tighter, to bring him back, and he started laughing. "There I go again!

I'm doing it again, aren't I?" And I said, "Yes, see how easy it is?"

Each time we went through these periods, Dad became a little more comfortable with the inner worlds. Soon he was passing between the inner and outer dimensions with ease. I began reading to him from the poetic Eckankar book, *Stranger by the River*. Although he had never been open to this in the past, he now listened carefully.

I told him to look for the spiritual guide in his new life. He might be dressed in blue, I noted, for this is how the Mahanta can appear in the inner planes. We talked about moving toward the Light at the end of the tunnel—into his new life. I was surprised he was so open to these concepts, because we had never spoken before about these things. The love of the Mahanta surrounded us in those moments.

On the last morning of Dad's life in this physical world, I sat on the edge of the bed and looked at him. Inwardly, I knew it was time. Quietly, I rose and went to find a nurse. I asked her to check his vital signs. She began to argue that she had just been in—that he was fine. I asked, "Please, won't you come in one more time?"

Finally she agreed. After she checked my father, she turned to me and apologized, "You're right. He is beginning to wane."

I sat on the edge of the bed and took his hands in mine. Looking into his eyes, I said, "Daddy, it's time. Are you ready?"

"Yes!" he said.

"Are you afraid?"

"No, Honey, I'm not now," he whispered. I began to explain that now was the time to close his eyes and gaze gently into his Third Eye, between his eyebrows, watching for the Light of God. I opened my heart to Spirit and asked the Mahanta to be with us.

Quietly, I explained that I too would go into the other worlds via a Spiritual Exercise of ECK. As Soul, I would meet him on the other side. There would be family and friends that he hadn't seen in a long time waiting to welcome him.

I leaned over and told him about the wonderful ECK word for God: HU. "I'm going to sing this word in your ear, and you can listen to the music of it. Very gently, you can put your hand into the Mahanta's hand and, with the sound of HU, float across to the other side." I held his hands, and sang the HU into his ear.

He began to breathe rhythmically, each breath becoming softer and more gentle. Around the eighth or ninth breath, the sound of his breathing was barely there, and finally it stopped. I sat back and noticed that he had the sweetest smile on his face. Then I closed my eyes, and my husband and I just sang the HU for a while. When I opened my eyes, I realized that my father had just translated, and I cried with happiness for him.

The nurse stood silently beside us, with tears in her eyes. Later, she approached me and looked very deeply into my eyes. "If only we could all go like that!" she said.

All at once, I felt privileged and yet very humble. At a time of great need I was able to listen and surrender to the workings of Divine Spirit. With gratitude, I realized that one of the greatest gifts of life is simply watching the spiritual force, the ECK, in action.

3

Spirit in the Workplace

We all reflect the Light of God.

Maestro, a Little Traveling Music, Please

Dan Kusnetzky

My flight to Houston was uneventful. With a yawn, I reviewed the manual for the new computer-communications system I would be installing when I arrived. My seatmates were busy discussing the current financial health of the airline, but it didn't strike me as an important topic.

Upon arrival, installation of the system went without a hitch. Each time I went to a remote site, the communication lines to the central computer worked the very first time. This network is coming up easier than any I've ever installed, I said to myself. But a small voice kept nagging at me. The Inner Master was trying to tell me that something about this whole trip wasn't quite right. But I couldn't put my finger on what it was.

The computer network was up and running; all the users had been trained. The nagging feeling didn't go away, but it was time to leave for the airport.

I arrived early, with plenty of time to return the rental car, check my bags, get my boarding pass, and sit down at the airport restaurant for a pleasant, relaxed meal. As I paid for my dinner, the hostess said, "Have you heard the rumors? The airline I was ticketed on was supposedly going out of business. Trying to be pleasant, I mumbled something about not paying much attention to rumors and headed toward the gate.

The airline had declared bankruptcy while I was enjoying my dinner. Upon hearing the news, many of the employees had left; their paychecks had already bounced for the last two pay periods. The airline had my ticket and my bags—and it seemed there was no way to get them back. How was I going to get home?

After experiencing the obligatory moment of panic, I did a short spiritual exercise. The Inner Master, Wah Z, told me to walk to the ticket counter, get in line, and wait for the return of my ticket. If the ticket had been purchased from a travel agent, other airlines would honor it. Since my secretary had arranged for my tickets, I didn't know whether a travel agent was involved or not. Wah Z's quiet inner voice said, "Don't worry, the ECK is with you. All will be well."

While I waited in line, I talked to the Inner Master, which helped me keep calm. This calm was noticed by my fellow travelers, and soon we were having a spirited discussion on the Law of Cause and Effect. What had caught us in the middle of this nightmarish situation?

After an hour and a half, my ticket was again in my hands. I was directed to go stand in another long line to receive my bags.

Since most of the employees had left over an hour earlier, the airline management had to empty the planes, sort out the baggage, and return it to its owners. This process was further hampered by Texas state marshals. They were impounding the planes to prevent the company's property from leaving the state. After another hour and a half in line and another spirited discussion on the Law of Cause and Effect, I had my bags.

Now that I'd assembled all of the pieces, I was ready to find a flight home on another airline. By this time, most of the flights and local hotels were already full. Wah Z's calm voice said, "Don't worry, you'll get home. Try to be cheerful, as a service to others."

I found myself in a group of stranded travelers, roaming from one airline ticket counter to another looking for a flight home. Finally, we found an airline that had a few seats left.

After a scramble, I stood in the waiting area, the hard-won boarding pass in hand. I heard Wah Z's quiet voice tell me to offer my seat to an elderly man who had come too late. Upon hearing my offer, the exhausted gentleman lit up like a beacon. When I accompanied him to the ticket counter to change my flight arrangements, the attendant asked both of us to wait. Were we both going to wait all night in Houston?

After everyone else had boarded, the agent turned to us. "You've been so friendly," she said, "I want to help you get home." We both left the gate clutching boarding passes for first class!

What a wonderful flight home! The elderly gentleman and I chatted for almost three hours about the laws of Spirit and the benefits of following one's inner guidance.

While driving home from the airport, I reflected on all the miracles that helped me to get home: my ticket was valid, my bags were found and returned to me, I found an airline that had a seat, and my seat was in first class.

The Mahanta had conducted it all like an orchestra, bringing in just the right elements at the right time. I laughed and said to Wah Z, "Maestro, a little traveling music, please!"

Being Love in a World of Power

Mark Bowman

There is a battle raging in my life between love and power. Often it is played out at work. How can I keep my heart open to Spirit—especially when working with others who wield a sword of power?

As an engineer, part of my job is to make sure our construction projects don't run over budget. One day I spotted a problem. I walked into my boss's office and suggested we avoid changing managers midproject. This would maintain continuity and keep job costs under control.

Immediately he assumed a defensive posture and said, "Close the door. I want to talk to you about this."

As I obeyed, I knew my approach had not been tactful. In a very ominous voice my boss said, "Are you saying I'm not doing my job? Because if you are, I take serious exception to that." I was in a corner, facing the death of whatever rapport we'd developed. Responding with facts and details would only fuel his anger.

Instead, I paused for a moment and looked within. "Mahanta," I silently asked, "why did I bring this up?" As I felt the presence of the Inner Master, my ego faded into the background. Facts and figures dissolved in my mind, and I was filled with nothing but the purity of my true intent.

In a soft, calm voice I said, "My only desire is to help. I want to offer my services so we can find new ways to avoid these losses."

He barked, "Are you saying I haven't already set up the means to do this?"

Again, I went within. With the Mahanta's help, I again tapped into the simple purity of Soul. "No, I'm not," I said. "I just want to help prevent cost overruns."

In the next moment, I saw the mask of fear lift from his face. He said, "Oh, OK," in a very matter-of-fact tone.

"Good," I said. I was free to go.

I was a bit shaken after leaving his office. But in that moment of confronting power, I had remembered to consult the Inner Master and surrender the results. I was happy with the outcome.

Two days later when I came in to work, I found a favorite pastry sitting on my desk. "Who brought me this?" I wondered aloud. I walked around asking all my co-workers, finally coming to my boss.

"Oh yeah," he said. "I remembered you said you liked French crullers, so I got you one."

Seeing a sparkle in his eyes, I simply smiled and said, "Thanks."

As I walked back to my desk, I realized the cruller symbolized a certain kind of love that had been freed in our business relationship. My boss and I had much more to work with now as a team.

The relationship I have with my fellow employees is rare. Each time I work with someone, I watch to see

86

how they will respond to what is offered. Will they react with love or power?

In high-pressure conflicts involving lots of money and prestige, I often serve Spirit as a silent channel. I simply open myself to the Inner Master and follow his guidance. Sometimes all I can do is entrust the situation to the ECK. Even so, my emotions can get tossed about, leaving me a little ragged by the end of the day.

When I come home from work feeling worn out, I sit down and contemplate, looking into the eyes of the Mahanta. All I see is endless love. In that moment, I know I am love too, and the passions of the mind fade. Castles of power may stand as part of the outer world. But as Soul, I know they can be filled from within by shining love for Spirit.

Breaking Limitations
and Discarding Fear

Larry White

Recently I was hired by the president of a fairly large company; he was impressed with my work for a rival firm. I was lured by those magic words, "You'll have your own computer—and real money."

After a week in my new office, I decided the money was OK (what money isn't?) and the computer was great, but the telephone was definitely a problem. It rang off the hook.

"Could you please help me with a job? I need it right away." Sure, no problem. "The deadline for this proposal was yesterday—can you finish it?" I guess so. "If this client doesn't get his answer now, the whole deal will fall through!" You don't say.

These calls from fellow employees wouldn't have been so frightening except I had a job to do too. A deadline screamed at me from the top of every project on my desk—most just days away. If a deadline was missed I not only had to face the people who signed my paycheck, but angry clients as well.

I soon discovered what the problem was. I was the only person in the office who knew how to operate the computer and one of the few who could successfully run the microfilm machine. So here I was trying to get my own work done, while others constantly needed my help. Soon I started getting interruptions in the middle of interruptions. There were so many that I sometimes sat at my desk with a stare as blank as the wall in front of me, having forgotten what I had originally set out to do, what my name was, what number came after two. Things looked bleak.

The fear of missing crucial deadlines began to eat away at me. I took the fear of failure home with me— not only to my apartment and family, but into my subconscious mind. I began to get more and more anxious as fear strangled my energies. There was no peace, not even in my sleep. My dreams were as jumbled as my so-called waking state.

Finally I decided to consult Spirit. I lay in bed with a pen and open notebook nearby, closed my eyes, and asked the ECK, What spiritual principle must I master to help me with my job?

Immediately I got the answer and repeated it aloud to myself over and over, very slowly: "Tonight I will be neither for nor against anything. That is the spiritual principle I must master. I am a channel for the ECK." Then I slipped off to sleep.

The next thing I knew, I was climbing flight after flight of stairs to reach a classroom. I was afraid I wouldn't get there on time; and the more fear I had, the faster the steps multiplied before me. Finally I gave up running. As soon as I did, an elevator appeared.

Suddenly I became aware that this was a dream. I was in a Temple of Golden Wisdom on one of the invisible planes. Whenever I realize I am dreaming, I try to ask Spirit, What can I do for you? So as I stepped into the elevator, I yelled, "What can I do for you?"

The elevator doors opened into a spacious room where a tiny Chinese man stood waiting. He sported a long white goatee. Luminous brown eyes shone from a thin, wrinkled face. Immediately I recognized Lai Tsi, the renowned Chinese ECK Adept. He handed me a coil of white string and said in a soft whisper, "See this wall and the wall opposite?"

I nodded.

"In the center of each wall, six-and-a-half feet from the floor, you will find a small hook. Please tie one end of this string to one hook and the other end to the opposite hook."

This wasn't hard to accomplish, and as soon as I had finished, Lai Tsi asked with a faint smile, "Do you enjoy painting?"

Here's the catch, I thought. The ceiling needs a new coat of paint, and I'm going to have to balance myself on this string, juggle a couple of cans of paint, and paint with the paintbrush clutched between my teeth. Weakly I replied, "I used to dabble a bit."

"Good," he said. "I have a little job for you."

The Chinese ECK Master vanished from the room for a moment, then reappeared holding a gigantic blanket of deep maroon. "You can help me unfold this," he whispered.

I took one end, and we began to unfold the cloth until it extended from one side of the room to the other. "Now help me drape it over the line," he instructed.

When we hung the cloth over the string, it formed a solid maroon curtain. Lai Tsi brought me several buckets of paint, a bucket of water, and a set of brushes, explaining, "Tonight there is going to be a special class for Arahatas [ECK teachers] in this room. Nine ECK Masters have volunteered to paint a mural on that

91

wall." He turned and pointed to the wall which was now hidden by our maroon curtain. Already I could hear paintbrushes plunging into buckets and splashing into action. "What we need from you," he said, "is a mural on this wall."

"Oh?" I croaked.

"Is there a problem?" Lai Tsi asked solicitously.

"Well, uh, how much time do I have?"

"Time?" He laughed. "Who cares about time? Just be done when they finish their wall."

"But there's nine of them!"

"That's why we put up the curtain, so they wouldn't bother you," he said calmly. "From what we understand, you prefer to work alone."

Lai Tsi left me to stare at the blank wall in despair. It's not fair, I muttered to myself. They're halfway done, and I can't even think of what to paint. What should I paint? Come on, man, think! Do they want the whole wall covered? Oh, I'm not going to get it done in time!

Just then, Lai Tsi opened a door on my side of the room. I could hear the murmur of voices in the hallway. "Just checking," he said. "The class is ready to enter as soon as the paintings are done."

He shut the door, and I stood frozen in terror. Hundreds of Souls were waiting for a class. What was I to do? What if I started painting and the ECK Masters suddenly finished their mural? My wall would look better blank than smeared with some halfhearted brush strokes. How did I get myself into this situation?

Suddenly it again dawned on me that I was dreaming and was to be neither for nor against anything.

"Need some help?"

I turned around to see Sri Harold Klemp, the Living ECK Master and spiritual leader of Eckankar, standing near me with a handyman's toolbox in his hand.

As I explained the situation, he surveyed the surface of the wall at close range. "Well," Harold said matter-of-factly, "before we do anything, we have to get all this rust and dirt off the wall."

"Rust and dirt?" I asked. "Where? I don't see any."

"Take a closer look," he said.

Sure enough, when I got closer to the wall I could see what he was talking about. "Oh, that won't hurt anything," I said hastily. "Besides, we don't have time for that!"

"It won't take long," Harold replied calmly. He opened his toolbox and handed me a scouring pad. I was about to protest when it again dawned on me that I was supposed to be neither for nor against anything.

Harold poured a bottle of soap into a bucket of water, and we began scrubbing and scrubbing. Whenever I thought we'd finished, Harold would point out another missed spot. I kept repeating softly, "I am neither for nor against anything."

Time was running out, I could feel it. When we finished scrubbing all the missed spots, I immediately headed for the paint. Simultaneously, Harold reopened his toolbox. Very nonchalantly, he announced, "Now it's time to polish."

Whoever heard of polishing a wall? Oh well, what's the use? I thought. I am neither for nor against anything. I am a channel for the ECK.

We polished and polished, and the more I placed my attention on letting things just *be*, the more I relaxed. As Paul Twitchell wrote in *The Flute of God*, "We must

93

enjoy the state of a calm and untroubled mind, in order for Spirit to use us as a channel. This state can be reached by passing beyond the range of the happenings of the moment and this can be done by the discovery of our immediate relationship to the source of all good." The gentle, melodious sound of a flute began to flow through my heart and mind.

"Do you think we've polished enough?" asked Sri Harold.

As he spoke, Lai Tsi returned from the hallway and pulled back the maroon curtain, announcing, "Open the doors for the class!"

As the students poured in, the ECK Masters' luminous painting filled them with awe and love. And its reflection in the highly polished wall opposite was so overwhelming it took their breath away.

Harold looked into my eyes and said, "Remember this. One must first be able to mirror truth, before truth can be unveiled to him."

The next day before work, I had two jobs overdue from the day before, several that were coming due that day, and countless interruptions. But each time I was pulled away from my work, I said to myself, "I am neither for nor against anything. I am a channel for the ECK." And whenever unwanted fears began to intrude, I imagined Harold and me scrubbing them off the mirror of Soul.

Fear sets limits. I've discovered that with less fear one can accomplish more work in the name of the SUGMAD for the good of all. Recently I was promoted to a position I had not expected for many years. As Lai Tsi says, "Who cares about time?"

Releasing Hidden Fears

Gloria Lionz

L ast month I had a dream which showed me how I let fear run my life. For weeks I had been asking to be released from any attitudes or patterns which were limiting me. I worked on this question each night before sleep with an exercise from *The ECK Dream 1 Discourses* by Harold Klemp. In the exercise I imagined meeting my spiritual teacher.

Suddenly, there was Harold Klemp, sitting calmly in a chair. He handed me reams of paper filled with information and said, "Well, you have a lot of fear. Here it is, all catalogued and ready to read."

The stack of paper was so high, I just looked at it. "I don't want it," I said. "It's too much."

"Well, you've been asking about your fears, so I thought you'd appreciate having a copy of them all. Here they are, in chronological order. All the fear you have ever experienced in all your lifetimes," he said, as he handed the mountain of paper to me with a light-hearted smile.

After a few rounds of passing the papers back and forth (I didn't want to read them), my teacher set the stack on the table between us, commenting in parting: "I'll just leave this here so you can refer to it any time you want to."

For some reason, I woke up from that dream feeling great. I knew that I had a choice. If I wanted to know more about letting go of fear, all the information I needed would be available in my daily experiences. I decided to go forward with my inner exploration of fear.

There followed a very hectic and upsetting week at work. I develop the budgets and balance the books for two large contracts held by my company. A large potential budget overrun in one of the contracts came to light, which I reported in a memo to the higher levels of management.

To put it mildly, they did not accept my evaluations. There was much gnashing of teeth and finger pointing about my abilities. As a perfectionist, I usually respond fearfully to any insinuations about my skills. But this time I remembered I was facing my hidden limitations. "This is a valuable experience," my inner voice whispered in contemplation. "Let's see what there is to learn about fear from this."

I was surprisingly undefensive as I went through various interrogations up the ladder of my supervisors. I even found myself saying, "Yes, I could have made an error. Let's check the procedure I followed and see if there is something I could or should have done differently."

I took my managers through each step of my reasoning process to reveal the budget overrun. As I talked, they seemed to calm down. Finally the person at the top—the one responsible for the contract—spoke up. "Gloria," he admitted, "I blew it! You did everything that was supposed to be done in this matter."

I had to check what I had heard, because such clear communication doesn't often occur at my workplace. But he even restated his admission at a meeting with others that afternoon.

This time there were a lot of managers I'd never met before. I had never before been included at this level of decision-making. The session began with a lot of anger and blaming. I was truly shocked at how little composure these top-level executives displayed.

After about fifteen minutes things calmed down, and my manager turned to me. "Gloria, what do you think our true situation is here?" I just about fell through the floor. I had simply come to the meeting as a budget supporter. Now I was being asked for some kind of summarization!

I gathered my wits and passed around a hand-written analysis of the situation. It was something I'd done on my own to better understand and possibly help the situation. That little piece of paper became the focus for true resolution. After another fifteen minutes, everyone agreed to go back to their offices, think things out, and come up with a way to solve the issue the next day.

All during this experience the words from a popular song kept dancing through my head: Don't worry, be happy. My spiritual exercises and a persistent feeling of adventure (after all, I was conquering some of my deepest fears) lent me an inner peace that far exceeded what my co-workers considered normal. I simply felt a connection within that overcame the hysteria around me.

After a few calculations the next morning, the manager called me. He said, "Don't worry, Gloria—be happy. We found the money to fund your people through the rest of the contract." I just chuckled and thanked the ECK once more for leading me through a maze of potential fear (and equally lethal flattery) with a good sense of humor. My defensive, perfectionist, and fearful days may be coming to a close!

A Life of Love

Rolf-Christian Müller-Uri

I work at a bank. Often I have a chance to observe an interesting co-worker who is a stock consultant. He lives by his own principles of love—though he meets considerable hardships.

When I started at the bank, I was impressed by the care he had for his customers. In a consultation, he took the time to get to know the individual—then followed his intuition in recommending an investment. Never did he push a client. Some took losses in following his advice, but the great majority doubled or tripled their investments.

The positive attitude he brought into the workplace attracted an equal degree of negativity. Almost constantly, he had to work with people whose single purpose seemed to be to ruin his status at work and bring chaos into his life. This included his superiors, who prevented any promotion for eighteen years.

Nevertheless, the consultant continued to create a kind of paradise in his part of the office. Wonderful flowers grew beside his desk, despite the fluorescent lighting. Every morning, he thanked the flowers for their petals as he watered them. For a year and a half, he even had a cricket living behind the wooden office wall, and the soft sound it made was very pleasant.

When I met him, he had just returned to the office from vacation, to find all his flowers had been thrown away. I spoke with him soon afterward about Eckankar. We talked about impersonal love, the love for all life that doesn't care what it gets back. He was happy when he realized that he wasn't alone in wanting to give love to the world.

I don't know whether or not he will act on his interest in Eckankar. But a short time after we talked about the spiritual exercises of ECK, he told me of a clear Soul Travel experience. In it he had flown over the Himalayan mountain range and seen a mountain shining like a huge white pyramid in the distance.

Knowing this man has given me a greater understanding of what surrender and endurance mean. By giving love and gratefulness to all life, one can find true happiness—despite all resistance.

A Meeting with an ECK Master

Ed Adler

Just when I think I know what a spiritual person is, life throws me a curve ball. Take Freddy Messier (not his real name), for example. Here's someone most people, including myself, would never have thought of as a candidate for profound spiritual experience. But he was.

Closely following a philosophy he may have borrowed from a well-known commercial, Freddy lives his life with great gusto. Fortyish, slim, and tall, slightly stooped and generally unshaven, he has suffered more than a little because of his great enthusiasm for colorful living. Even a serious digestive illness hasn't been able to hold him down for long. He loves having fun.

Sometimes Freddy's fun is not so funny. He loves to tell the most creative and outrageous stories you can imagine. If you bite—and most of the time you will—he really enjoys your discomfort when you discover just how gullible you've been.

He can stir up trouble at work, pitting one person against another. But probably his greatest delight is sharing a seemingly endless supply of jokes with the ladies at work. Whenever there are both loud squeals of laughter and grunts of dismay rising above the background hum of knitting machines, I know Freddy is at it again. Some really enjoy his humorous style, while others are shocked and offended by it, but that doesn't stop Freddy.

That's the side of Freddy most people see.

He has another.

It's warm; it's loving. Sure, he doesn't demonstrate it much, but some of us know it's there. I first discovered this when a fellow worker, a woman who is loudly critical of his ribald storytelling, found herself in a personal crisis. Her life seemed to be falling apart all around her. One particular day, feeling completely overwhelmed, she began to tremble violently and then disintegrated into hysterical sobbing—right on the assembly line. All work stopped as we ran over to find out what was happening. It was Freddy who got there first and, without a moment's hesitation, firmly held her shaking shoulders and then cuddled her in his arms and comforted her as though she were a baby. We all stood there frozen—just watching. Amazed.

Freddy was now gently whispering to her, "You'll be OK. What you're going through is only temporary. It'll pass. You'll see. Let it go. Let it go." He gently stroked her hair, and when her shivering began to subside, we knew she needed no other help but Freddy's.

In a short time she was quiet. She later told us that it was Freddy's kindness and encouraging words that helped her through that time.

Then there was Freddy's exceptional relationship with his stepfather, Alphonse. After Freddy's divorce and his mother's death, he moved in with Alphonse. I had often seen Alphonse, a quiet, frail, gentle man with a wistful, sweet smile, sipping hot coffee at the lunch counter of a favorite restaurant. He usually ate alone; and he missed his wife terribly.

Alphonse was not Freddy's real father, but the bond of love these two shared ran very deep: They even looked alike. When the old man was critically ill and needed a lot of special attention, all his blood relatives seemed to melt away. Not Freddy. He was always there to bathe and feed the dying man, play cards with him, read to him, and when necessary, carry him from place to place. He cared for him tenderly, right to the end.

I had first heard about his stepfather's condition one day at work when Freddy told me that Alphonse was suffering from terminal cancer and was failing fast. He no longer had the strength to get out and drive to his favorite restaurant. He had barely enough energy to sit up in his chair at home.

What really puzzled Freddy was that Alphonse was now having very long, one-sided conversations with his deceased wife and other beloved relatives.

"You know, Ed," he confided in me, "these are real conversations. They make sense somehow. I can't see or hear the person he's talking to, but it sure seems like he can. The reason I'm telling you about this is that I heard you're into some kind of spiritual thing—what do you call it—Eckinbar or Akankar or something. So I thought maybe you could help me with this. Are those people really there, or is Pop just losing it?"

"Freddy," I said, "it's a religion called Eckankar, and no, I don't think your stepfather's going crazy. He's probably just getting ready to leave this life. Sometimes when someone is close to death, their focus here in the physical world starts to blur. They begin seeing and hearing loved ones from the other side, the Astral Plane or heaven. These loved ones can help them make the change. It's natural and not all that unusual. But I

103

am curious. What are the conversations like? Did you take any notes?"

"Well, no, I didn't. But it wasn't anything special. They were talking together about everyday things— just like they used to."

"If you get a chance," I suggested, "it might help to write down some of what you can hear on this end."

"I'll try," he said. But that was all I heard from Freddy until about two weeks later.

"Hey, Ed," he said, picking right up where we had left off. "You'll never guess what's happening with Pop now." He didn't wait for my response. "He's got a new friend—you know, the kind you can't see. When I ask him who this new guy is, he just tells me to mind my own business. I think Pop's afraid I'll scare his friend away or something. I wouldn't do that—Pop really seems to like this guy. What do you think? What's going on?"

"I have a hunch it's really important to find out who this new friend is," I answered. "Why don't you try again? See if you can find out who he is and what he looks like."

A few days later a grinning Freddy greeted me with a wrinkled scrap of paper with a few words scratched on it.

"Success!" he shouted. "Here it is—I wrote it down! His name is Tsooko Yen. At least that's as close as I can figure from the way Pop speaks English. He also said this friend was a foreigner or something—maybe Chinese—had a long, droopy mustache and was dressed in some kind of old-fashioned clothes. But what's really weird is Pop tells me this guy is giving him advice—like what to expect when he passes on."

A little tingle—a sort of "truth alarm"—ran up and down my spine, and I started to wonder. "It may be," I said, "that besides your mother and other relatives, there's a spiritual guide working with your father."

I was still puzzled, though. I didn't recognize the stranger's name. Who is Tsooko Yen? Could an ECK Master—someone I had never heard of—be helping Alphonse? There have been so very many ECK Masters in a long, unbroken line over the centuries. I knew the names of some, but many more were unknown to me.

Then I thought about the copy of Paul Twitchell's *The Spiritual Notebook* I happened to have with me that day. It was sitting on my desk, and I remembered there were names and descriptions of some of the ECK Masters there. Since Paul had included only the more prominent ECK Masters in the book, it would be a real long shot. I hesitated for a moment, but gentle intuition whispered, Take a chance. I invited Freddy to join me in searching through the appropriate chapter.

We scanned hurriedly through the book. The first time we looked, we couldn't find anything that matched. I closed the book. "Wait a minute, Freddy," I said, "maybe you wrote the name down the way it sounded to you. It could be spelled a little differently, couldn't it?" With that idea in mind, we tried again, and this time the following paragraph seemed to jump right out at us:

"The ECK Master Chu-Ko Yen was an associate of Confucius in China. He guided the Chinese Master by giving him spiritual advice in his work to reach the world and form a greater society. He passed on and became a spiritual guide on the Alakh Lok [the Sixth Plane of consciousness or heaven]."

Freddy and I were both stunned. We stood there saying nothing. I looked up at Freddy's face. The tension lines had started to ease; he suddenly looked younger, as if a great pressure had been removed from his heart.

"You know, Ed," he said, "I wanted so much to help Pop, to say the right things, but I'm not that good with words. I prayed in my own way for help for him—and here it is. You know, I really love Pop."

Freddy hesitated then; he stopped. He took a deep breath and regained his composure. He looked around, smoothed his hair with his hands, nervously cleared his throat, and suddenly walked away.

Sensing his apprehension, I didn't feel it was appropriate for me to run after him and tell him there is an American serving as the Living ECK Master. Harold Klemp is the present spiritual leader of Eckankar—actively teaching and guiding thousands of spiritual students around the world today—right now!

Freddy never said anything more about this unusual event, and somehow he made it clear to me he didn't want to talk about it.

My guess was he wasn't ready to deal with all the implications of an ECK Master befriending and guiding his dying stepfather. He must have realized it would require some drastic rearranging of his priorities and views of reality to pursue answers to all the unasked questions.

It's been about three or four years since his stepfather's death, and Freddy hasn't changed very much. Maybe he's quieter and a bit more thoughtful. He still tells an occasional off-color story, but he doesn't stir up trouble like he did before. Sometimes he walks by, and I feel he has something he wants to say to me, but he just smiles or tells a joke.

I must admit, I did wonder—why Freddy and Alphonse? What brought such an incredible blessing into their lives? I mean, neither one of them was on a spiritual path—but then I realized, maybe they were. They were completely unselfish in their devotion to one another. Maybe their special spiritual quest was unconditional love.

In Harold Klemp's recently published book, *The Living Word,* I found the following passage:

> Spiritual travelers routinely cross the borders of life and death; they travel freely into the heavenly worlds because they are agents of God....entrusting the secret of God to anyone who sincerely wants to overcome the fear of death....They may appear at the most unexpected times, but always to give a blessing, if one is ready for it.

The ECK Masters are here to help and guide more than a privileged few. They serve all of life.

4
Dreams: A Key to Life

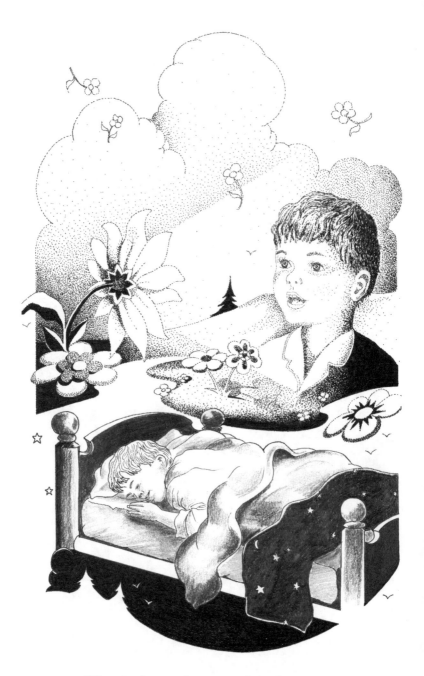

What is the truth we touch in dreams?

Dream Travel Can Make Any Job Easier

Rae Franceschini

Have you ever been so nervous or anxious about a new job that you almost quit before Day One? I had been at the same job for nearly nine years when I decided on a complete career change. Twelve-hour days pared down to six; five days a week down to three. The biggest change was going from sitting all day to standing.

The interview went well, and my new employer and I agreed on the day I was to start. But now, a whole new fear gripped me. How well would I do my new tasks?

The job was in a cookie store. I had baked a lot at home and knew how to cook, yet this was different: two large ovens, three tall racks for cooling trays of cookies, huge tubs for dough, and on and on. It dawned on me that each day we would be making nine different kinds of cookies. How would I master all this?

Immediately, I became very nervous. It wasn't long before I considered calling the owner to back out. Finally, as my fear peaked, I let my inner awareness surface long enough to say, "Hey, wait a minute! Give yourself a break. Put a little trust in your inner

111

guidance; you might be fine." I did stop fretting but wondered: Had that been *my* voice? Did I really believe I could do this job well?

By now it was late Friday night, time for bed. I set my fear aside and took a few deep breaths. I asked the Mahanta to help me cope with the days ahead and give me the inner strength to give the new job my best shot.

In the dream state that evening, the Mahanta took me to the cookie store. I knew it was late, but the lights were on and no one was there. In the dream, I started to explore the shop. I looked under the counters, opened drawers, and checked cupboards. I saw where all the paper goods were kept and the ingredients for making dough. I noted which supplies were kept in the walk-in freezer and how things were done. Getting familiar with the shop really set me at ease. I finished my night's sleep peacefully.

What an incredible opportunity I had been given. I awoke early Saturday with a clear and total recall, and immediately thanked the Mahanta. For the rest of the weekend, I didn't give the new job another thought. All I could do was my best, and after that, I could learn.

The following Tuesday was my first day. The person training me was really more interested in the fact that it was her last day. In her excitement, she reviewed my tasks too quickly. I watched and listened. When it was time for my trainer to leave, my other new co-worker became nervous. Was she going to have to do all the work alone for the day, with me in the way?

I saw the dread in her eyes as I set to work, pulling tools out of drawers and running out back for ingredients. I asked her to make dough, remarking that as soon as she had it done, I'd start dropping the cookies. I continued to arrange things in the store as if I had already been working there for many months, instead of hours.

She looked at me and said, "How do you know where everything is?" I said, "Sometimes you just have to trust your inner feelings. Now I'm really going to need your help, if we're to get all this work done today."

We started making cookies, and a few hours later we finished ahead of schedule. She was surprised but happy to have me working with her.

I left work with the most wonderful feeling. Thanks to the Mahanta, I got through Day One and took a giant step in self-confidence and awareness.

Accident: Will My Dream
Experience Become Reality?

Margaret Kramer

For the past two years, I have kept a dream journal. Upon waking I have recorded deep insights regarding my own life, glimpses of future events, and some seemingly nonsensical dreams with no clear meaning. I'm often tempted not to bother recording this last type of dream. But that attitude changed forever when one of my nonsense dreams not only came true, but showed me a path of action to take in an emergency situation.

The dream started ordinarily enough. It began with my stepson Charlie and me walking along a circular mountain path; he was somewhere close behind. Suddenly a huge boulder came bouncing down the mountain. I had just enough time to dive for safety, but as I watched helplessly, the rock landed right on top of Charlie, then continued down the mountain. I ran to him, but his broken back and twisted body held little chance of survival.

I scooped him up in my arms, wondering how I could ever carry him to the hospital. In a flash the scene changed. With Charlie sitting behind me, I was now guiding a tandem bicycle down a very steep hill to the hospital. As I pedaled, I realized he looked different. He no longer had dark hair and a young surfer's build but was tall, blond, and skinny!

As I became aware of this difference, the scene quickly changed again. Now I was in a busy hospital, frantically writing a brilliant red message to my husband. I was afraid Charlie would die before my husband could get here. The scene flashed again. My husband was walking the gangplank between two towering buildings still under construction. Hands reached out to him from the far side, but he stubbornly refused assistance. Trying to navigate the narrow plank, he finally took the waiting hands, and they pulled him to safety. I literally jumped out of bed — wide awake.

The dream made no sense. I felt Charlie had been heading for trouble lately, so I shared the disturbing dream and warned him to be careful that weekend. Since he was in his wild-teenager phase, I often warned him not to get in a car with a drunk driver or get mixed up with drugs — something he had shown too much interest in already.

My husband had been under an incredible strain from Charlie's antics already, so I said nothing to him, deciding that the dream was a graphic portrayal of the family's troubles.

Two days later, after midnight, I sat in bed unable to sleep. As the clock ticked past 2:00 a.m., I finally lay down to see if I could get some rest. I had barely closed my eyes when I heard a commanding voice shout, "Get up!"

I jumped right up! I recognized the voice of Rebazar Tarzs, the Tibetan ECK Master, although I had never consciously heard his voice before. As my feet touched

116

the floor, I heard a tremendous screech and a horrible crash. Someone began screaming, "Help me! Oh, God, somebody help me!"

Half-dressed, I flew out the door in the direction of this pleading voice. I found a young boy, dazed and bleeding from numerous cuts, kneeling in the street over a body.

People took action quickly. The boy, obviously in shock, was gently led away. The car accident was on a one-way street, and someone with a flashlight started rerouting oncoming traffic.

As I stepped closer, I saw the young man lying in the street was horribly injured. People were afraid to touch him. Kneeling down next to him, I felt an incredible power flowing through me. Suddenly, everything became crystal clear—he was the tall, skinny blond boy from my dream!

An electric energy pulsed through me, and I could feel the Mahanta close by, waiting for me to assist him. I don't recall my neighbors calling to me to be careful or any second thoughts about what I had to do. I had to help this young man face death.

His injuries and the fear of those around me no longer mattered. He was bleeding profusely from the neck, but I found myself leaning close anyway. I whispered in his ear, "Don't be afraid." At this point someone got up the nerve to take his pulse. When they were done, I continued. "Look for the Blue Light; see it? There's someone in the Blue Light. Go with him; his name is Harold Klemp. He is the Mahanta"

I reached out and lightly touched him on his Third Eye, in the center of his forehead. I felt like an observer. Some other powerful force was directing my every move! The words flowed of their own accord, like water.

"Go with the Mahanta; don't be afraid. It won't hurt anymore; take his hand."

As I spoke these words, there was a long sigh, and his rigid shoulders relaxed. The ambulance arrived, and he was taken away.

Looking through the crowd, I recognized his mother wandering aimlessly down the street in a bathrobe. She politely refused my offer to drive her to the hospital, saying she would walk home. "My son is always getting into these things. He'll be fine."

I didn't want to interfere, but I raced home and got my truck anyway. She was in shock. When I caught up with her again, she was all alone, walking up a steep hill toward her home. This time she didn't refuse my help, but I couldn't get through to her (or to her eldest son at home) that time was of the essence; if we didn't move quickly, the boy would die before we arrived at the hospital. They insisted on driving themselves and slowly went into the house to dress. Just like my dream, I was worried they wouldn't arrive in time.

Driving home, I carefully reviewed the dream and turned it over slowly in my mind, fitting the pieces together. The boy was blond. He had been thrown from the car, which then ran over him and continued down the street—just as the boulder had landed on him in my dream.

But in my dream I had taken him to the hospital! Should I turn around and go? Rebazar's voice woke me from my thoughts. "Go home!" he commanded.

Slowly I showered and returned to bed. Just as I was about to fall asleep, I heard a soft voice say, "He's on his way to heaven." I knew the boy had translated and that he was with the Mahanta.

The next morning, I learned that the young man's mother and brother had made it to the hospital in time for a last farewell. The Mahanta saved them from the pain and guilt they would have felt had he died before they arrived.

The facts later revealed that he was a problem teenager, not unlike my own stepson. The boy had done volunteer work that evening at the annual neighborhood luau, and he and a friend were rewarded with several beers before they drove the few blocks home. The neighborhood learned a hard lesson that night, and the practice of giving alcohol to teens ended abruptly with his death.

Shortly after the accident, my husband gave up trying to deal with his son by himself. He joined an organization called Toughlove that showed him how to cope with the pain, hurt, and frustration of a problem teen. With the help of other parents, I watched my husband's guilt finally dissolve. He now accepts that teenagers who know right from wrong are responsible for their own actions. It was a major breakthrough for us both.

When I think back to the night of the accident, I don't dwell on the blood or the sorrow of that accidental death, but recall instead how the Mahanta opened his arms of love to a young teen in great need.

Escape from the Pit

Ed Adler

Eckankar is a spiritual teaching which shows the individual the way back home to God. For me, that journey began with a mysterious dream just a few weeks after I had applied for membership in Eckankar.

"Somebody help me—please!" I cried in this dream. The stench around me was unbearable. Up to my waist in a steamy, foul-smelling cesspool of mud, I was horrified of sinking even deeper. Nausea beat through me in endless waves as I struggled to get out of the mess which held me with clawlike fingers. Could this be hell? I wondered. If it was, it was much worse than I had ever imagined. Never had I felt so helpless.

I struggled until exhausted, then stopped to figure out where I was. At first there was nothing but my fear and the darkness. By the light of a dim reflection from above, I could just make out a cavernous space that extended hundreds of feet above me. Somehow I knew I was trapped in the basement of a tall building.

As I looked around for help, I noticed someone standing against the far wall, near a bank of brightly lit elevators. He was a tall, slim, ebony-skinned young

121

man with a warm smile and piercing black eyes that gazed right through me.

"Why don't you help me?" I shouted. He answered by unfolding his arms and beckoning me to come toward him. What's this? I thought. He wants me to get over there by myself. But that's impossible! I'm really stuck.

I had nothing to lose by trying. Amazingly, I found the strength to struggle through the sludge to where he was standing. He reached down to help me up and out. I was finally free—at least from the noisome pit. Little did I know that my adventure was just beginning.

He didn't say anything, just pointed to one of the waiting elevators. It was the strangest-looking elevator I'd ever seen. There were no sides or top, just a plain wooden platform with an upright control lever. He stepped on the platform and nodded for me to follow. As I walked doubtfully to the strange contraption and stepped on, I noticed a young lady standing nearby. I don't know where she came from, but without saying a word she joined us on the elevator. Who is she? I wondered. I strained to see her face but inexplicably couldn't focus my eyes. Her features remained a blur. (It would be several years before I discovered who she was.)

Meanwhile, the silent young man pushed down on the control lever, and we flew up with amazing speed. In my waking life, I suffered from an uncontrollable fear of heights, and I was terrified as I looked down at the rapidly disappearing basement floor.

With great effort, I forced my eyes away from the dizzying space below to the serene face of our guide. How easily the icy fear melted away in the warmth of his quiet assurance. The mystery woman also seemed unconcerned about our swift ascent, and I relaxed a little.

Despite our great speed we climbed for a long time, higher and higher. Finally we reached the top and stepped carefully onto a flat, gray, gravel roof. The atmosphere was gray too. The heavy mist was an oppressive blanket which allowed barely enough light for us to see our next step. As we groped our way to the edge of the roof, I was very aware of the deep abyss only one step away. How I wished we had more light. Every cell in my body cried out for more light!

Without warning, our guide raised his arm and pointed to a spot in the blind gray sky where, from behind the leaden veil, he inferred the brilliant sun would soon be shining. He kept pointing.

I'm not sure how long we stood there like that. It could have been a split second or a thousand years. When the golden-white light exploded through the heavy sky, there was no sense of time. Every square inch of creation was instantly bathed in the loving light of truth. There was no more fear, pain, anger, jealousy, hate, despair, or loneliness anywhere! There were no boundaries, no separation—for all things had their being in the One. There was nothing to seek. All there ever was or would be existed in the here and now.

I yearned to remain in that glorious moment forever, but the beautiful vision slowly faded. It was morning, and I was sitting in my bed at home. Tears of joy and wonder flooded down my cheeks. Has this all been just a wild dream? I asked myself.

"No, of course not!" came the instant response from within. I knew this experience was a precious gift that would change me forever.

* * *

The next day, a letter arrived inviting me to a local Eckankar Satsang, or study class. I was filled with joyful anticipation. Somehow, I knew it had everything to do with my dream. The warm letter from the Arahata (teacher) informed me that the class was scheduled to meet in just a few days.

On a brisk January evening three nights later, I walked up to a large apartment house in a fine, old residential district of the city. I knocked softly on the front door, my hands trembling from more than just the chill wind. Already, a giant wave of joy flowed through the solid oak door. I hesitated a moment, frozen with the sudden realization that once the door opened, my life would never be the same. I shook myself and knocked once more — boldly this time, in an attempt to conquer my lingering fears.

The door opened wide. There stood a tall, slim, ebony-skinned college student with a warm smile and piercing black eyes. "Can I help you?" he asked.

My voice shook, but I managed to choke out, "Thanks, you already have!"

"Hi, I'm Al," he said quietly and invited me in.

I had a hard time looking at Al in class that evening. The golden-white light dancing all around his head and shoulders was so dazzling and brilliant it brought burning tears to my eyes. I thought, If this is what it's like to be with a teacher of Eckankar, what will it be like when I meet the Master?

It was an exciting and dynamic time of discovery and change for our small Satsang class, as we explored new inner and outer worlds each meeting. Al was a firm but gentle teacher, and miracles were becoming commonplace for each of us. Our class gradually increased in size over those early months, and strangers very quickly became loving family. When Marie joined us, there was something about her that made me wonder if we had met before. She was an attractive fair-haired young lady with blue eyes that saw deeply into the mysteries of Spirit. As we continued our studies together, I often thought to ask her if we had met before, but gradually the idea faded from my mind.

Sometime later, a small group of us were traveling together to an Eckankar workshop. The conversation shifted from the beautiful weather outside to an exciting discussion of our inner adventures. I was just beginning to describe my adventure in the cesspool when Marie stopped me. "Don't you know who the other passenger on the elevator was?" I must have responded with a blank expression on my face, because she continued, "That was me!" Then she proceeded to describe, with amazing accuracy, every single detail—from the wild elevator ride to the golden-white light bursting through the heavy, gray mist.

This story may seem like science fiction to some, but it is just one of many spiritual adventures shared by members of my local Eckankar Satsang class during the time we studied together. Where are the words to express our joy, gratitude, and wonder? Satsang is a vital channel—a way for Spirit to encourage and guide each Soul on the long journey back home to God.

How to Knock Down Fears

Larry White

*Anyone who has training can dream con-
sciously for when he dreams and is conscious of
the process, then he learns to see how this waking
state is also a dream. Just as in the dream state
any ECKist can learn to manipulate the environment, do anything he desires, simply by the
knowledge that it can be done. Also in this waking dream state he can do the same, when he
learns the techniques of doing it.*

—The ECK-Vidya, Ancient Science of Prophecy,
by Paul Twitchell

Dreams have helped me so many times that I can
hardly recommend a better way of talking to
God. A few years ago, fresh off the unemployment line,
I was hired to abstract legal documents and information for a real-estate title insurance company. I had
not been there long when my boss asked me to type the
insurance policies.

Little did he know I couldn't type in the generally
accepted way. I had my own method, which boiled down
to every finger for itself. To show him I was eager for

new responsibilities, I hit my keyboard so fast on that first day that even Bach would have been impressed. I was very proud until my boss began finding typographical errors. "Been to an eye doctor lately?" he asked, not totally ecstatic.

The next day I slowed down a little and made no mistakes at all. My boss got very agitated. "Is that all you've done? Here, take this!" He handed me a bottle of Geritol, a popular energy tonic. "You need it more than I do," he said. I was beginning to feel frustrated. My fingers were flying so fast the next day, I thought the typewriter keys would melt. But the harder I tried, the more mistakes I made. Finally I yelled, "This is driving me crazy!"

My boss looked up and quipped, "Short drive."

As usual, he proofread my work at three o'clock. At four, he wasn't upset as he had been all week. He just asked if I knew anyone who wanted a job.

I had to do something quickly. Man cannot live by bread alone, much less no bread at all. When I got home, angry at myself and fed up with life, it dawned on me that all week long I had not been paying the slightest attention to my dreams.

I decided to take a shot in the dark. That night, as I lay in bed, I said out loud, "Dreams, I'm having a serious problem, so serious in fact, I don't even know what it is. I just can't seem to do anything right. If you can help, I promise to listen." To let my dreams know how serious I was, I laid a pen and open notebook at my bedside to write them down.

That night, I found myself in a bowling alley, of all places. A bowling tournament was underway, and here I was in front of hundreds of spectators, not to mention

TV cameras, doing something I had not done more than three times in my entire waking life.

Immediately, it was my turn. The first two throws were consistent: both went straight into the gutter. The crowd roared with laughter. My turn to bowl came up again and again.

"A strike!" I would say to myself. "I've got to get a strike!" But the harder and faster I threw the ball, the quicker it tumbled into the gutter.

Of course, all the other contestants had been bowling since their first lifetime on earth. I was ready to give up and go home when the Living ECK Master, Harold Klemp, appeared beside me. He held a pair of binoculars.

"Here," he said. "I think you may need these."

"Very funny," I said.

"Don't be afraid," he replied. "Take a close look at those bowling pins."

He offered me the binoculars, and I took a peek. Sure enough, here was something I hadn't noticed before. Inscribed on each pin was a particular fear. One said, "Fear of Failure." Another read, "Fear of Ridicule." Another, "Fear of Rejection." Others included "Fear of the Unknown," "Fear of Making a Mistake," and "Fear of Not Being Absolutely Perfect." I turned to Harold and said, "These are the very fears I have been struggling with all my life."

"Really?" he said. "Well, here's your chance to get on top of the situation."

"How?"

"Very simple. Just imagine how you would honestly feel, on the surface and deep down, if these fears were cleared from your path. After all, they are really

129

nothing more than dead images from the past, no more alive than those bowling pins."

"Thank you," I said, stepping up to the alley. When I picked up the ball, he said, "This is the ball of conscious thought. See the middle path?"

I looked down the alley to see a series of brilliant blue arrows running right down the middle. In the center of these arrows ran an almost invisible golden thread.

"Just release your conscious thought to the middle path and be neither for nor against what happens, for then you are truly trusting the ECK."

I released the ball to the straight and narrow, and bingo—a strike! Harold handed me a snapshot of the bottom of a shoe. Suddenly, I heard the piercing sound of a flute and woke up.

I was grateful for the experience, but the ending left me on edge. I began writing the dream in my notebook, but when I came to the picture of the bottom of a shoe, I was completely baffled.

After I recorded the sound of the flute, my intuitive response was to reach for *The Flute of God,* by Paul Twitchell. I grabbed the book off the dresser and just "happened" to open to this passage:

> You should have a good picture of the Real Self, the individual that is really you—Soul.... You must not let outer circumstances get so much of your attention and activity that you cannot pause, take time and lean upon the ECK Power.... You are a part of the Divine Power so your thought forms a mold which the power instantly fills with life. Therefore, what you think with the whole of you, on the surface and deep down, inevitably comes to pass and manifests.... Belief in Spirit can take care of all things in the outer life. Life can be so relaxed, that it is a joyous possession. Many millions trust in Spirit and find the fulfillment of all their dreams.

From that day on, I was no longer Larry White, Mad Typist Desperate for Approval. I was simply Soul, the calm and fearless dreamer of isness, hereness, and nowness.

At first, I still made my share of mistakes, but when my boss commented on them, I viewed him as Soul and realized that, in a way, he had been seeing me as Soul all along. He had been aware of my full potential and now had motivated me to see it for myself.

I took my attention off making mistakes and placed it on just being Soul—working only for God, for the good of all. I learned the difference between pleasing people out of insecurity and serving the SUGMAD (God) out of sincerity. Whenever fears popped up, I imagined they were nothing more than bowling pins and started throwing strikes. The less I feared a mistake, the fewer mistakes I made. Within a few weeks, I got a raise and was promoted to full-time policy typist.

As Rebazar Tarzs, the great Tibetan ECK Master, tells Paul Twitchell in *Dialogues with the Master,* "When you have destroyed fear, you find you are really one with the ECK, and when you consciously can realize this power by practical demonstration of your ability to overcome any adverse condition by this power, you have nothing to fear."

No Fear of Dying

Ben Hunter

In 1979 I had a dream within a dream which changed my view of death overnight. At the time I was very unhappy and wanted nothing more than to run my life into the ground and be done with it.

In the midst of this despair, I was given a book written by Paul Twitchell which was the only light in my otherwise darkened world. After reading it I had this dream—if truly it can be called such, for I have no recall of falling asleep that night. As soon as I lay my head on the pillow, I stepped into the midst of another life.

I could recall another childhood with different siblings and a complete set of memories, hopes, and dreams leading to that present moment. I was in the intelligence branch of the British Army, in World War II. Crowds surged in the streets as I hurried unnoticed down the less-crowded back roads to a prearranged rendezvous.

Climbing the stairs of the appointed building, my thoughts turned to the recent events of the war. I was vitally interested in what new strategy would be laid before me behind the closed door ahead. But when I saw their plan, I was speechless with anger. I was to impersonate an enemy informant in a meeting with a key Nazi officer. It was madness, for I knew the officer was far too familiar with the man I would impersonate to be taken in. But I had no choice. I had my orders and would fulfill them the best I could.

When I arrived the next day in the clearing that was our appointed meeting place, the officer was waiting for me with a dozen armed escorts. As I approached, our eyes locked, and immediately I realized that he knew I was an impostor. I turned and fled. His soldiers gave chase as he barked commands.

I ran for the woods on a small path covered with pine needles. As I crested a small rise, I tripped and fell, protected momentarily by the hill. I had no time to think, however, as bullets flew.

I jumped up and whirled to face my attackers, who were less than forty yards away. Two soldiers fired simultaneously, rifles clutched to their hips, striking me in the stomach and chest. As I fell, I began to leave that body. Then my viewpoint shifted back to the ground for a moment. As I looked out of the eyes, I saw only the ground all around me. But at the same time I was aware of an overview, as if this whole forest were the stage of a theater, and I was the director peering down from above.

I felt the footsteps of an approaching soldier and watched from above as the commander directed him to finish me off. He placed the barrel of his rifle directly under my right armpit and pulled the trigger.

The bullet dove into my body like a diver through multicolored waters, taking my consciousness with it. All else was gone now, as image after image hurtled by: Queen Victoria, regiments in red coats, lives in Rome,

Greece—back further and further in time until finally there was only a stream of orange-and-yellow-and-gold light.

I finally came to rest. First, in a place where I seemed to be lying on black rocks by a black ocean with the waves pounding me under a black sky. Then this too faded, until I was only a thin line of beingness stretched from here to there, with no thought in between but the feeling of lying on my back and on my stomach, on the ceiling and the floor—all at the same time; none more than the other.

There was no body and no thought; no images to grasp, but still there was beingness. Then there came a twist, a snapping of this thin line of consciousness that sent a ripple the length of my universe. I wanted nothing more than to remain in this place, but this was not to be. As the impulse rolled through my being, I moved with it and was sent spiraling down, back toward the human state of consciousness.

I awoke with a start and sat straight up in bed, drenched with sweat. The shock waves continued to roll through me as I became—as if for the first time—the person I am now. The experience, and the expansion of consciousness it brought, was too great to hold in my human awareness.

Overwhelmed, I got up and headed for the bathroom. As I walked shakily down the hall, my brother poked his head out of the next room. He rubbed his face sleepily, but his gaze was sharp as he asked, "You OK?"

"I guess so," I said. "Go back to sleep." He shambled back to bed, and I returned to mine.

Now I entered another state. The next thing I knew, I was again suddenly awakening in bed with the first experience of awakening vividly impressed on my mind. As I reviewed each scene, it all began to feel more like a dream—until I came to the sequence with my brother. Then a tingle went up my spine. My brother was not next door, but thousands of miles away in northern Africa.

I knew then that I could never cease to exist. Death was only a transition from one life to another and could provide no escape from this life. Whatever problems I faced would surely follow me, life after life, until I worked them out as Soul. As I sat quietly in bed, I became aware of Paul Twitchell looking down at me from outside my window as the dawn broke over the tops of the trees.

You see, his look seemed to say, this is the way it is.

And I did see. With the fear—and hope—of death removed, there was nothing to do but get on with life and solve its mysteries.

5
Stories of Healing

Healings from the ECK come in many different ways.

A Test of Courage

Mary Carroll Moore

The summer I discovered I had cancer taught me much about fear—where it comes from, and how it leaves the heart and is replaced by love.

The removal of my fear began with a routine blood test. I had been feeling tired, and at my checkup I asked the lab to run a thyroid panel. The numbers showed possible malfunction of the thyroid. On the advice of the doctor, I made an appointment with an endocrinologist.

The specialist dismissed the blood-test numbers but was immediately curious about my thyroid, which protruded slightly on the right side of my neck. "What's this lump on your neck?" he asked. I shrugged, "Oh, it's been there for years. Probably from a car accident; the muscle's strained." "Not a muscle strain," he said. "I'll be right back."

He stepped out of the room and returned with a lab technician. "This might be a tumor," he said. "We can perform a biopsy right now and see what the tissue looks like."

Later that week, I called the clinic for the results.

"The tissue shows abnormal patterns. It could be cancer," my doctor said. "We'd like to do a radioactive scan on the tumor. Can you come in tomorrow?"

My mind was awhirl. I was seeing my life change before my eyes: death, disease—my worst fears were being realized. Cancer, I thought. Oh, my God.

I closed my eyes and desperately asked for help and guidance. The reassurance came from the Inner Master, "I'll be there. Go ahead with it."

I asked the doctor for some time to think this over. His parting admonition was not to take too much. The scan later that week showed a good possibility of a malignancy, and an operation was advised.

The ECK, or Holy Spirit, was beginning to stir depths of myself that I had been afraid to examine for centuries. I shook inside for days, as one dire possibility after another surfaced.

My mother suggested flying to Baltimore, Maryland; the family had friends at Johns Hopkins Hospital. We would find the best surgeon, the best oncologist. The wires hummed between Baltimore and Minneapolis almost every night, as my family rallied to my support. The event was causing a vast healing on all levels: we were closer to each other than we had been in years.

The day of the surgery I was in a daze. Feeling the Inner Master quite close, but with my palms sweaty with fear and my throat an even bigger lump, I was wheeled into the operating room. I joked halfheartedly with the anesthesiologist that I would be his best patient. That was the last thing I knew.

I found myself in a beautiful city in another world. All my dreams had come true. I had somehow escaped all fear, pain, and death. A young Adonis romanced me. He said he loved me and wanted me to stay forever in the lovely place he had created. In return he promised to take away all the fears that had clouded my life on earth. The inner world was huge, light, and happy; people lived by creating music and art instead of working. It seemed as though I had everything, but a thought kept intruding: Where was the Mahanta, the Inner Master?

The young man showed me the place where I would live. I was entranced by the spaciousness, the lovely feeling.

At one point I put my hand in my pocket and was surprised to find a folded slip of paper. I knew the Mahanta had written two words on it. They were two things I loved very much in my life on earth. Not easy things, but things that were helping me work out my fears and grow stronger. Although it was the more difficult road, I knew that in my earthly life I was experiencing great tempering of Soul.

It was tempting to stay in this place of beauty and light, where I knew no fear, but I had to return to earth to complete the work I had begun. This was my choice.

Reluctantly I told the young man I had to go back. He protested and tried to keep me; I realized later this was my struggle to reenter the physical body.

Although only hours had passed, it seemed like days. I was floating above my body as it lay in the recovery room. I knew I had to go back, although it took all the effort I could muster to move my hand and slowly come back to consciousness.

Later my mother told me it had taken hours to revive me in the recovery room. I had been so pale and deathlike. She never knew how close to the truth that was.

All night I struggled with the choice I had made. The world where my fears had miraculously dissolved seemed even more appealing now. Dying seemed a positive choice when my body was so full of pain. Everything hurt, and I was nauseous from the anesthesia. My throat felt empty, as if more than a cancerous tumor had been removed. The loneliness of returning to this gray world was overwhelming.

But the Mahanta had been there all along—not visible, but in those two written words. I later came to understand that the heaven I visited while my body lay unconscious was in the lower planes; the young man had tried to trick me into settling for less than my destiny. My sense of obligation to return, to work out my fears, had saved me from a beautiful trap.

It was not until months later that I began to piece together the puzzle of this event. I felt like a weight had been removed from me and also that I had passed a test of courage. Now I have gained a chance to reach a much higher heaven than that which the beautiful young man had offered me.

But the greatest gift of all from this experience was the removal of something deep down that I had not even noticed until it was gone. Fear.

Fear is a tricky thing. It can arise from long-buried experiences in another life or a childhood trauma. It colors our actions and reactions, controlling us in subtle ways. From fear, negative attitudes such as anger and jealousy can grow. Still, we hold on to our fears like old overcoats, believing they protect us from an alien world.

For me, it took a life-shaking event before the human self would allow the fears of the past to be dissolved in the ECK stream.

The young man in my vision had promised to remove my fears—the easy way out. By choosing to re-

main and face my fears, they have been removed in a
more complete way.

Three Hospital Miracles

Sherry Witcher

What happens when an ECKist enters a hospital? In my experience, almost anything can.

I will start with 1973 when I gave a young man his Third Initiation in Eckankar. This ECK student was stationed in Japan with the U.S. Navy when he received a notice that he was eligible for his next initiation.

Initiations in ECK are given only by those who are in the Fifth Circle of Initiation or above. So as soon as he returned to the U.S. for a short visit, the ECKist phoned to request my assistance. He didn't have much time ashore in San Francisco, and I was scheduled to be in Saint Luke's Hospital for surgery on that date. I said if he didn't mind coming to the hospital, I would initiate him; so this he did.

When the young man arrived, he drew the curtain around my bed for privacy. He didn't realize that the lady in the next bed was paralyzed—she could hardly interfere. She had suffered a stroke and could not even speak. Yet all during the initiation, I sensed some kind of activity on the other side of the curtain, although no one had come into the room.

145

When the young man left, to my amazement, my roommate raised her head and asked, "Who was that tall, young man?" By evening, the paralysis was completely gone, and she was healed of the stroke! She left the hospital before I did.

In 1979, I entered the hospital again, this time with my neck in traction. When I arrived the other bed was empty, but soon a young lady with a broken knee was brought back from surgery. She was in agony, biting her lip to keep from crying out. So I said inwardly, "SUGMAD, if that young lady would like help, please let it be given to her."

The next morning, when her doctor came in, he found the surgical incision healed. She had perfect mobility in her knee! The doctor, of course, was amazed. She was released from the hospital that same day.

Finally, at the end of 1980, I had to go into the hospital for a third time. During my stay, a young ECKist got a pink slip for her Second Initiation and wanted to receive it on New Year's Day. So again I said, "If you don't mind having me do it in the hospital." She said she would come.

I explained to the nursing supervisor that I was a priest in Eckankar and a lady was coming who needed a spiritual consultation. She allowed me the use of a room right across from the nursing station. Of course, as always, there were many ECK Masters present during the initiation and a tremendous amount of power built up in the room.

When I opened the door after the initiation, a blast of power surged out. The young lady was standing behind me, so I don't think she saw what happened. Right in front of the door there was a gurney blocking our way. On the gurney was a body with a blanket

146

tucked in all the way around, which meant the person was dead. When I saw that, I said, "Oh, SUGMAD!"

Immediately, moans started coming from under the blanket. One of the men who had been pushing it exclaimed, "I guess we'd better uncover him!"

When he lifted the blanket, I saw a beautiful teen-age boy, who turned his head and looked at me. His eyes were bright and sparkling. I smiled, and he gave me a big smile back.

Now do you know why I say anything can happen when an ECKist enters the hospital?

A Spiritual Healing

Jean Adcock

Two years ago, I was told I had cancer. My doctors performed a double mastectomy, the removal of both breasts, and placed me on radioactive cobalt treatments and extensive chemotherapy. It wasn't my first bout with this dread disease. Ten years ago, I had survived cancer of the digestive system and vocal chords.

This time, I decided I would deal with my cancer in a new way. I would face it squarely and discover its cause.

I was doing OK until I started to lose my hair. Then I began to despair of ever being well again. One afternoon when my spirits were especially low, I was confronted by a small child. In a loud whisper, he asked his mom why that lady didn't have her hair. The mother looked down and laughed, and said, "Why don't you ask her, Son?"

I told him I had been really sick. "The medicine I have to take has something in it my hair doesn't like, so it all ran away."

With a child's knowing smile, he looked up at me and said, "I guess my dad had to take some of that same medicine, because his hair is running away too." The small joke helped me make it through my next chemotherapy treatment.

Then my doctor told me, "Things aren't going as they should, Jean; you're not getting better. I'm sorry to tell you it's just a matter of months." I was going to die.

On the way home, I decided I *wanted* to die, even at the risk of going somewhere unknown after death. The doctors stepped up my treatments to twice a week, but my health continued to decline.

About this time, a little voice inside me piped up. Over and over it said, "You remember that nice woman you met, named Irene? Go see her."

It repeated the message until I had to find this Irene. "I've only met her once," I protested. With a sigh, I got up and put on my shoes. At that moment a knock sounded at the door. To my amazement, it was Irene!

"How are you, Jean? I felt I just had to come see you." I poured my heart out about my health, my hospital bills, and a lot of other things. I cried until my eyes were swollen.

Finally she took a deep breath and started talking about a spiritual Master, the Living ECK Master, who always helped her when she was in a tight spot. She spoke of Eckankar and the Light and Sound of God, the ECK. Suddenly a clear picture of this Living ECK Master flashed through my mind. Could it be? I asked if she had a picture of him.

As she pulled the small photograph out of her wallet, I was startled to see the face of a man I had seen in my dreams for years!

"I didn't know he was your Master too," I said to Irene. "I remember he tried to help me, but I pushed him away. Do you think the Living ECK Master would help me now?" The rest of Irene's visit passed in a blur. Only one thought pulsed through me: "Please accept and help me, Mahanta."

That was ten weeks ago. I am studying Eckankar in a local Satsang class, and I am healing. My doctors are so amazed they've ordered weekly X rays to document my progress.

Last week, after carefully scanning the latest X rays, my doctor admitted, "Somebody up there really likes you." I just smiled and replied, "Yes, they do." He turned to my husband. "I just don't understand it. I've heard of miracles, but this is my first in forty-five years of medical practice!"

I know the Inner Master is the force behind my healing. I don't need radioactive cobalt treatments anymore, and the chemotherapy will end in a few months. The doctors are cautiously talking about a complete recovery. But I know the Mahanta has already healed me!

Finding a Heart of Gold

Julie Olson

A s a child of twelve, I had a dream. I was standing in the cemetery near home. One by one, I looked at the children's graves—flat marble slabs the size of shoe-box lids lying level with the ground. Suddenly I spied an intensely bright gold coin glittering in the dry brown grass. As I stooped to pick it up, I saw other coins scattered in an abundant trail across the lawn. I collected many of them to take home, feeling rich and full of glee. As I picked them up, the trail of gold coins led me out of the cemetery. The dream ended.

The next day, I went to the graveyard after school, half-hoping I'd glimpse a gold coin. The dream stayed with me but had no real meaning until almost twenty years later.

* * *

In September of 1986, an unchecked infection raged through my kidneys and bloodstream. My husband and I were living in a new section of our large city, and my

153

physician was out of town. When my temperature reached 106 degrees, my husband took me to a hospital that offered emergency care.

The next four days were a nightmare. The hospital was overcrowded and understaffed. (It later came under federal investigation for incompetent care.) The doctor was unfamiliar with my medical history and couldn't diagnose my problem. I developed a life-threatening case of pneumonia that went completely undetected. I lay in the hospital approaching death, surrounded by medical knowledge and technology.

Each day I thought: this can't get worse. But each day it did. The improper care, ineffectual medicine, and overcrowded room were all part of a carefully crafted plan. It wasn't apparent at the time, but I was right where I was supposed to be.

I was never quite conscious. Instead I felt myself hovering around or above my physical body, not wanting to feel the constant pain and discomfort. Having studied the teachings of Eckankar for fourteen years, I never lost that all-important link with the Inner Master. The illness and pain seemed to take all my attention, but the loving presence of the Mahanta, my spiritual guide, wafted in and out of my consciousness. It gave me great comfort and security.

However, I began to ask Spirit why I was not getting proper medical attention. What had landed me in this crazy hospital? My husband and parents were becoming alarmed. I didn't have the strength to lift my arm. It was hard to breathe. Clearly I was near death. I felt helpless and weak, too ill to demand anything. I couldn't even focus my attention enough to chant HU, the ancient name for God. Occasionally just the *H* and *U* would flash together in my inner vision like a neon sign.

On the fourth morning I began to sink. I could actually feel myself loosening the grip on physical reality. I stopped struggling at that point and surrendered. "Anything is better than this, Mahanta. If I am ready to leave, I will go." My mind cleared for the first time, and an inner calm descended. It was clear I was very close to translating (dying). My body felt like a broken, feverish husk, no longer useful. And yet I felt a powerful current flowing through that part of me that was not physical. Soul was calm, peaceful, observing, and detached.

As I moved beyond the pain of the body, I recognized a familiar, floating feeling. I'd felt it many times before during the Spiritual Exercises of ECK. I was out of my body—perhaps this time never to return. I kept saying to the Inner Master, "I am ready, I am ready." I felt no emotion, no pull toward family or loved ones— just calm expectancy. So this is dying, I thought.

Then, as if someone had suddenly flicked on a movie projector, I saw a scene from the classic movie, *The Wizard of Oz*. It registered in absolute clarity upon my vision—every note of the music perfectly pitched and clear, every detail in vivid color far beyond the reaches of Metro-Goldwyn-Mayer.

Dorothy finds the Tin Man rusting away in the woods, locked into one position as the years passed. She had just oiled his joints, and the sheer joy of movement makes the Tin Man dance. I watched every nuance of the Tin Man's movements, felt every musical note, as pure happiness animated his clunky body. His joy was unhampered by the awkward shell he wore.

The Tin Man's song was "If I Only Had a Heart." He pleads with Dorothy to take him to the Land of Oz, so he can ask the Wizard for a heart, since his creator

155

forgot to give him one. Every word of the song registered deeply. The scene faded at the end of his song.

As I returned to my physical body, the tears rolled down my cheeks. *I* was the Tin Man—encased in a hard shell of physical, emotional, and mental rust. This rust was karma—a shell of pain that had built up through lifetimes of heartbreak and disappointment. Now it was keeping me from my true heart—as Soul.

I asked the Inner Master to help me open my heart to Spirit in this life. Only the ECK Life Force could soften the karmic rust of centuries. I saw that this rust had collected over many incarnations, dating as far back as Atlantis. My heart had been broken many times, as I failed important spiritual tests.

The scene changed, and I was standing in a mist. Something began to take shape before me, and I became aware of a large, round table. I seated myself at the table with several of the ECK Masters of the Vairagi Order.

Sri Harold Klemp was immediately recognizable, as were Rebazar Tarzs and Fubbi Quantz. A discussion commenced. I couldn't hear the actual words, but there was a vibration or hum which signaled their conference. I knew the conversation was about me. Presently the discussion stopped, and a question entered my consciousness: "Julie, what do you want to do?"

A feeling of great love, patience, and compassion surrounded me as their question sank in. Did I want to leave the physical body now? The choice, as Soul, was mine alone.

Two thoughts cropped up so quickly my mind didn't have time to censor them. Soul, the observer, was speaking. One was concern over my husband's anguish and pain. We'd been married only four months. The second was: I haven't yet met the Soul who just joined our family, which is very important to me. (My sister had just had a baby.)

At that moment my fate was sealed. There was no opportunity to mentalize the choice; it was made beyond the mind. Soul, the Golden Heart, had made Its choice. I felt a sudden surge of purpose and strength as I returned with a rush to my body.

Things moved quickly after that. Within an hour my regular doctor phoned. I was released into his care at another hospital.

The ambulance ride was a lonely one. I felt the weight of my decision as the reality of the physical universe closed in around me. The bouncy ride, the wailing siren, the narrow gurney I was strapped to—all stood in stark contrast to my spiritual visions of the morning. I felt painfully alone. Ironically, a deep fear of death clutched at my heart.

Just then, the ambulance attendant began to sing. Softly at first and then louder, part lullaby and part hymn. I immediately felt the presence of the Mahanta and relaxed. I couldn't see the attendant (and for all he knew I was unconscious), but his soothing voice drowned out the wail of the siren. His unself-conscious song carried the healing force of the divine Sound Current. I'm so weak, I thought, I couldn't ask him to continue should he stop. But he didn't.

When we arrived at the new hospital, I was caught up in a whirl of activity as my body was hooked up to various machines and tubes. I remained in the intensive care unit for three weeks. It took a full twelve months to regain my health completely. The Living ECK Master declared that the Year of Spiritual Healing for the chelas of Eckankar—and many other searching Souls.

*   *   *

The childhood dream of golden coins returned and stayed with me. It was a promise made long ago by Spirit. In this life, Soul would be freed by the Mahanta from the dead traps of ignorance. The karma of many lifetimes would be dissolved—lifetimes where I had lost all resonance with myself as Soul.

Each golden coin in my dream symbolized a secret gift from the ECK—a key insight into life. These insights would lead me out of the constant round of birth, death, and rebirth, out of the physical plane (the cemetery). Soul was free of Its earthly bonds.

Eckankar is the path I have chosen to help me gather the golden coins of wisdom in my path. I have the deepest gratitude to the Vairagi Masters and especially to Harold Klemp, the current Living ECK Master, for showing me how to use them to open myself as Soul. I guess you could say the Tin Man found his heart of gold.

The Mahanta's Healing Ways

Alfred Dorais

A little over a year ago, I went for a routine physical exam at the Veterans Administration Clinic in Orlando, Florida. They diagnosed me as having two polyps in the lower intestine. They weren't large ones. The doctors said they would watch them.

A year later I went back for another exam with a different doctor. He verified that I still had two polyps in the lower intestine and scheduled an appointment for possible surgery. The polyps had increased in size and were possibly cancerous.

That evening, the Mahanta whispered an idea: It is possible, as Soul, to heal oneself in the dream state. So I did a spiritual exercise and asked the Mahanta, Wah Z, if this were possible. I caught a glimpse of him as he nodded his head in the affirmative. I knew I could expect further nudges for a healing soon.

The night before I was to enter the hospital, a technique flashed into my mind. The Inner Master gently introduced a suggestion: Catch yourself at that point just before you fall asleep—between waking and

159

sleep. Imagine yourself bathing in a healing orange light.

I tried the suggestion. Just as I was about to drift off to sleep, I caught myself and visualized the physical body being immersed in orange light. Humbly I asked the Inner Master, "If it's for the good of all concerned—and doesn't interfere with my spiritual growth—would you please take the polyps away?" I drifted into a sound sleep.

The next morning I drove to the VA hospital with peace in my heart. Two doctors examined me. They consulted with each other and then said, "You can go on home, Mr. Dorais—the polyps are gone." There would be no operation.

To me, this simple healing proved the validity of the Eckankar teachings. I feel it's important to note the disclaimers in my request: "If it's for the good of all concerned—and doesn't interfere with my spiritual growth." That way, if we're ready for a gift from the Inner Master, it will come.

A Deadly Race against Time

Debra Kaplan

A few months before attending an ECK World-wide Seminar, I had a disturbing dream. In the dream, I was at the seminar, running to the main auditorium. I opened the doors and looked inside—and every single person in the auditorium was in a wheel-chair! When I woke up, I couldn't figure out the dream, but I faithfully recorded it in my dream journal anyway.

Life went on, and about two months later, my husband offered to buy me a very nice weight-lifting machine. I accepted his offer, and two men came out to set up the machine in my home.

It turned out that the proper handlebar for the machine was missing. The installers gave me a bar from an older machine, saying, "It'll be OK. Use the old bar, and as soon as the new one comes in at the shop, we'll send it out to you."

They left, and I started to try out the machine. Within the first five minutes the handlebar they had given me slipped from the machine. My foot was almost completely severed from my leg.

For one long moment, time stood still. As I stared at my leg, I saw Wah Z, the Inner Master, standing next to me. Without words, he told me it was OK. This "accident" was a result of karma from another life; I would be all right.

Things happened quickly after that. The ambulance I called whizzed me to the hospital. As the surgeons reconstructed my foot, they told me that I was very lucky to have survived. But, as Soul, my attention was directed to the deeper reason for this event. I had to know why. What karmic tie had brought about this horrible accident? I asked the Inner Master if I could see a fuller picture of the true cause-and-effect relationship at work in my life.

I discussed some of my dreams, which held the clues to my injury, with a Higher Initiate in ECKANKAR. As he listened, the picture became clear.

The karma that caused my injury was with the two men who had delivered and set up the machine. Two lifetimes ago, I had caused them similar misfortune which led to their deaths.

I, as Soul, had chosen this lifetime to repay the debt for that transgression against the spiritual laws of life. As I looked further at the Akashic records, it was clear that the accident was originally destined to conclude this lifetime. But the Mahanta had interceded on my behalf.

On the path of Eckankar, one can begin to work off tremendous amounts of karma in the dream state and through the daily Spiritual Exercises of ECK. Unwittingly, I had been in a race against time. But through the grace of the Mahanta, the Inner Master, enough of the karmic load was lifted so the accident didn't take my life.

Looking back, I realize that I had had a burning desire to study Eckankar for three or four years before I became a member. Now I know why. I was racing against an internal clock. I have five small children; it would have been hard for them if I'd left this life so soon. Now I'll get to see them grow up.

I also understand my wheelchair dream—since that's my mode of transportation these days! However, I'm very hopeful I will one day walk again. I'm forever grateful to Wah Z for giving me the protection and help necessary for me to stay in this life—for more spiritual lessons, love, and growth.

Awakening the Spiritual Eye

Ravi Jaisinghani

I t had been a difficult night for my wife, Anita. She was almost seven months pregnant and had had stomach pains the whole night. But they were different than labor contractions, so we decided to continue with our usual routine. Early the next morning, we each left for work.

About 9:00 a.m., Anita called me from work. The pain was getting more intense. She planned to visit her doctor immediately and then go home.

Her doctor suspected a low-grade urinary infection but was cautious about prescribing antibiotics during pregnancy. She suggested rest unless the pain intensified. However, the pain continued, unabated. Finally, in the afternoon, the doctor prescribed an antibiotic from the neighborhood drugstore.

Meanwhile, I had inwardly asked the Mahanta that if it was the will of the divine ECK, I would like to help my wife. I closed my physical eyes and focused on the Spiritual Eye, between and slightly behind my eyebrows. For many months I had been practicing the

Spiritual Exercises of Eckankar, which teach one how to look within via this Third Eye.

Now, as I looked gently at the inner screen, I saw transparent sheets that looked like clear plastic wrap. They were peeling away with great energy from my body and flying toward Anita. But instead of clinging to her, they returned to me. I heard the inner voice of the Mahanta say, "They are dead."

Perplexed, I looked at the sheets of energy more intently. Instantly, I understood that these were protective wrappings to me, but they held no power or healing comfort to help my wife's karmic situation.

I had planned to visit a police bicycle auction directly after work. Anita called later in the afternoon. The pain continued, and the prescribed medication wasn't improving the situation. She suggested that I still go to the bicycle auction, since returning home early wouldn't necessarily make her pain go away any faster.

At the auction, I bid on a lady's bicycle and also bought one for myself. I returned home feeling quite happy about purchasing two bicycles, eager to tell Anita about the bargains.

But as soon as I opened the front door, I saw my mother and Anita preparing to leave for the hospital. The doctor didn't want to delay diagnosing the pain any longer. We all left for the hospital in the family car.

I drove to the emergency entrance and left the car in a temporary parking zone. Feeling the gravity of the situation, I sped my wife through the admittance process. Anita was wheeled to a room in the maternity ward.

Her doctor took me aside. The acute pain could be attributed to kidney stones, gallbladder stones, or a urinary infection, but it was difficult to diagnose because X rays couldn't be used during pregnancy. Meanwhile, the pain intensified, and Anita was writhing on the hospital bed.

The doctor started Anita's physical examination, and I rushed out to move my car from the temporary parking spot to a longterm parking space. Luckily, I found an empty space very close by. I was running back to the hospital, when a young man stopped me. He was dressed in a woolen jacket and scarf appropriate for the mild weather.

He asked me for fifty cents, explaining that he didn't have quite enough money for taxi fare to take an injured friend home. I asked to see his friend, since no one was nearby. He called out, mentioning that his friend and girlfriend were across the street behind a parked van, but still I couldn't see anyone.

Confused as I was by the suddenness of this odd request, my intuition suggested this might be a spiritual test or opportunity. After a timeless moment, I gave him the fifty cents, and he thanked me. He called loudly to his friends. Moments later a tall man limped out from behind the van, supported by his girlfriend.

As soon as I had given the man the money, the Mahanta spoke reassuringly from the inner realms. By making an unknown stranger's journey less painful, the same could be done for my wife. Not realizing the full impact of this blessing, I rushed back to the hospital. There I found Anita in a relaxed state; her pain was quickly diminishing.

Being skeptical by nature, I still didn't believe what the Mahanta had said. I asked how the ECK could remove something like a kidney stone so quickly. The Mahanta lovingly and simply explained that all material things exist in temporary states. All temporary

167

states are subject to change. Material objects, like kidney stones, are also subject to change.

A few minutes later, the doctor returned, saying Anita's urine sample seemed to have black specks in it, like very fine stone dust! There was no more pain. Though two more specialists were called in, they were equally perplexed as to what had caused the acute pain and its sudden disappearance.

I recorded this experience in my journal and showed it to Anita a few weeks before the birth of our daughter, Ajna. Now, while writing this story, I realize that the name we gave to our daughter is more than a coincidence. *Ajna* is an ancient word for the Third Eye. It lies between the eyebrows, a doorway to the spiritual worlds. It was through the experience at the hospital that I knew my Spiritual Eye was being awakened.

6

Developing a Golden Heart

Expressing ourselves is God's love in action.

Cooking with Love: A Spiritual Recipe

Mary Carroll Moore

I perched on a high stool, watching my class of seven adults who had come to learn about cooking. Introducing myself, I asked Joseph, an engineer from San Jose, why he chose to take this class. "I work with computers all day, talk the lingo of machines to everyone I work with," he smiled. "I need to feel something alive—a bunch of celery or rising bread dough."

As the weekend of classes progressed, Joseph blossomed in other ways than just his cooking skills. The quiet, nervous engineer with awkward movements became a gentle, friendly individual who enjoyed the easy classroom banter. No doubt, the celery and other foods were doing their share of inner healing.

From the hundreds of Souls who pass through my cooking classes each year, I learn more and more about the spiritual side of cooking and food. It is more important for overall well-being than most of us know. It involves our families, friends, and our own self-awareness. Most people have yet to learn the art of feeding themselves and others, both outwardly *and* inwardly—the art of giving love through food.

Peggy, a housewife in her late fifties, was in my cooking class to gain confidence. All her adult life she had been cooking for her husband and children. When her first loaf of bread come out of the oven, she was transformed.

"That's mine! I can't believe it."

I was touched by the beauty of the moment as Peggy held the bread like she would a baby. Cooking had always been a duty, but now she was seeing how to nourish herself too. Nourishment came inwardly when she put love into her cooking.

Another example is Douglass. Douglass is a chef at a small California restaurant. He and his small staff cook in a kitchen that feels like a temple. I learned that his reverence for food came from witnessing a family miracle.

When Douglass's wife was paralyzed in a car accident, he became her full-time nurse. He believed he could help her heal herself. Good food, lovingly prepared, became the way he expressed his faith. His wife was subsequently healed by the power of love.

To watch him at work is like watching a sculptor with his clay, a priest reciting devotions, a musician playing a sonata. Eating the appetizing creations Douglass makes always awakens a reverence in me— the same reverence he puts into preparing the food. Love through food is a praiseworthy way to express Spirit. After all, everyone eats.

Working with my students has shown me that cooking is truly an art. Like all art forms, it can lift both creator and receiver to a higher state. I feel this myself when I cook dinner for close friends. Filled with the anticipation and excitement of making something for people I love, I choose ingredients with care and spend many loving moments on my masterpiece—transported to a higher place. I share food with those I love; of course, it tastes wonderful—how could it not?

We put love in food for our loved ones, but what about when we cook for ourselves? Some days when I come home, I feel a need for something I think is in the refrigerator. I fill my body, hoping to fill that need for love. But the principle is: To get love, you have to give love. When I come home from work grumbling, open a few cans, and get no satisfaction, it's because I haven't put any love into my cooking for the Soul that is me.

Food is surely a medium for love, both here and in the other worlds. In fact, sometimes food is used as a poor substitute for love—for what we can't find within ourselves. I once read about eating certain foods for comfort. Many people have their own comfort foods which they eat when they have the blahs (or need more love): toast with layers of butter, bags of chips, chocolate, ice cream, even baked sweet potatoes.

The search for love through food is all around us. I advertise that I teach cooking, but what I am really teaching people is how to love themselves more. I help them energize their food and nourish themselves by cooking. They become more open to give and receive love—the essence of Divine Spirit. You can cook for yourself and others, and learn the power of love. It's the force that nurtures all.

So a new spiritual exercise emerges: a chance to experience a greater awareness, to Soul Travel, to be a clearer channel for Spirit—all while nourishing the body. I tell myself that I am partaking of the pure essence of the ECK as I eat my hamburger: "This meal is an expression of love from Spirit. I will receive all the love I need, as I relax and eat this food."

Thus the temple is created and it becomes my kitchen, and eating is a spiritual experience unlike any other.

Is Your Pet a
Spiritual Weather Vane?

Karen Walasek

C arolina, whom our family lovingly called the Rat Dog, had a long snout with whiskers that appeared ridiculously long for her face. When we got Carolina as a puppy, we thought she was a Labrador, but our "Labrador" didn't grow much bigger. In time we grew to appreciate her size as quite convenient for traveling and curling up at the end of the bed.

Carolina had a habit of knowing when one of the family was coming home. Soon we began talking inwardly to her miles before arriving home, imagining Carolina waking from her sleep and preparing our greeting. Carolina took her duties quite seriously. They included guarding our son, Justin, and making heroic attempts to replace his cries with chuckles and smiles. Family arguments couldn't last long while the Ridiculous Rat shivered and quaked at our harsh words.

Carolina was a constant reminder to keep our attention on Spirit, the positive, neutralizing force in our lives. Often we would be caught in a whorl of negative emotions, only to look at Carolina and dissolve with

175

laughter. Our Ridiculous Rat was very good at her job.

Of course, as with any relationship, she had her annoying side, but often these annoyances were educational. I remember sitting one night at the dinner table with my fork poised at my lips. I was having an inner conversation with myself on how full I was and decided it would be best to feed the rest of my food to Carolina. Instantly Carolina jumped up and pranced around my chair with hopeful eyes and a swiftly wagging tail.

"Rats! The least you could do is wait until I've said it out loud. Just for that, forget it, I'm not giving you any." I scolded her and put another bite into my overloaded stomach. It startled and frightened me that this little black beady-eyed dog could snatch my thoughts. Sure, we always joked about her knowing when we were coming home, but this was different. This was undeniably real. As my fear retreated, I realized that Carolina had not invaded my mind, but was once again a barometer for reality. I was creating thoughts, and she was merely receiving them.

Carolina never understood our emotions, but she definitely took steps to eliminate problems. If I was upset, she would lay her head in my lap and wait patiently to be recognized. My introspection would slowly reverse and become an outward demonstration of love. This little furry messenger of God showed me a gentle way to let go and switch my attention to higher things.

Some will laugh when I call my dog a messenger of God, but in her own way Carolina was the purest and swiftest path to my heart. She would even help me with the Spiritual Exercises of ECK. Not only was she easy for me to visualize on the inner screen, but she helped take the tension away. As I sat down to chant HU, my mind would start yammering about my terrible voice. This made me tense, but then Carolina would start howling. She put her whole heart into it, completely absorbed and unself-conscious. All I could do was laugh—at her, at me, and at the seriousness of it all. Soul is a happy entity. Soul Travel is fun. Even a little black dog knows that.

One night Ron, my husband, and I returned home from an Eckankar discussion class to find the house unusually quiet. Carolina didn't come pounding down the stairs (as much as a little dog could ever pound) in her usual manner. When I found her lying under the bed, I had the fleeting thought that Soul was no longer in the body. Although Carolina didn't seem to recognize us, she struggled to her feet and ate and drank a little. She always did this as part of her greeting ritual, but this time every move she made was automatic, as if she were somewhere else.

Morning found Carolina's condition worse, and we bundled her off to the veterinarian. He said she'd had a stroke and promised to call us immediately if her condition changed. We wanted her to die at home if possible.

Suddenly, while driving home, Ron complained of feeling dizzy. I immediately noticed a tingling numbness between my eyes at the Tisra Til, the Spiritual Eye. It didn't take much discussion to drive straight back to the vet. Carolina's breathing was labored; it was obvious that she had waited as long as she could. Through eyes blurred by tears, we all petted her while Ron quietly gave her permission to leave. We all chanted HU. Her breathing slowed, then stopped; her heartbeat faded. We were honored that she waited for us to see her off. Although the experience was painful, we all had grown up some on this path to God.

Carolina had been our barometer, teaching us how to recognize and control our emotions. She taught us many things, and now it seemed her job was done. We didn't need her anymore—it was time to take responsibility for ourselves. She still shows up in our dreams or on the inner every now and then to quake at an angry word or to greet us at the door; but she doesn't have to listen any longer when I tell her to guard the house. She's free to go wherever she chooses or wherever her next mission takes her. I heard her the other day as I chanted HU and felt warm all over. I thanked her once again for her gift of love.

The Spiritual Art
of Relationships

Nancy Landon

Ten years ago I married the love of my life. It was a beautiful sunrise ceremony, and I felt the total bliss of spiritual and human love. We had chosen bright silver wedding bands to symbolize the joining of our love and our lives. They were thick and wide, and our ring fingers felt heavy with them on.

A few days passed, and my new husband and I noticed the skin beneath our rings was beginning to suffer. So we began removing them each night so the air could reach the skin and allow it to breathe.

We didn't see how Divine Spirit, the ECK, was trying to tell us that we needed space in our togetherness. For many years we blindly believed that the love we felt on our wedding day was all we needed for our marriage to survive.

Eight years into the marriage, trying times fell upon us. One cold December night my husband asked for a divorce. I was devastated. In the cold blackness of the night I cried out: "Why?"

A still voice within me, the voice of the Mahanta,

answered: "You have lost compassion for your husband."

Stunned, I knew it was so. I had ceased to give him freedom—the space to grow and bloom. The message of the rings from so long ago echoed in my mind.

A few days later, with respect and love, we removed our rings and began to live apart. It was not easy, but it did feel lighter. The divorce became a reality.

I wondered, What is love? for I no longer knew. Once a friend told me, "Love is seeing the good in another and letting the rest go."

I had always known that and applied it to others, but not to my family—those I loved most. The Mahanta told me, "You will learn to love him in a higher way."

Another friend told me of a culture which did not allow the exchange of wedding rings at the time of marriage. It was thought to be a display of ownership, and no one could own another. Did I own my husband? Did I own that relationship? Certainly not now.

Several months later and half a continent away from our old life, my beloved and I decided to try to rediscover the love we once knew. It has not always been easy.

The wedding rings sat in a box on the dresser. Occasionally I would take them out and look at them. One day they were gone. We discovered they had been stolen by a neighbor boy who had sold them.

They were gone for months, then one after the other they reappeared. Somehow, the neighbor boy got them back. Spirit was telling us something: This time we would make it.

We are learning that the sustenance we sought from each other can only be gained from God. When I sit quietly and sing the ancient name for God, HU, I feel the love of Divine Spirit and see the good within myself, my mate, and all life. My priorities are now in order.

Last night I asked my husband, "What is love?"

He replied, "It's certainly different than I used to think it was. To me it is sharing."

And we are.

What I Did for Love

Debra Roy

The nurse held up a test tube, visually checking the color of the contents. I caught my breath and felt my body suddenly chill as she announced: "The results are definitely positive." Her words fell heavily upon my ears. I was pregnant.

For many people, this news would be the cause of joyous celebration. For me, it was the opposite. Fresh out of high school, I was looking forward to the college education I'd just begun. This was a serious setback. I took time to carefully consider my options.

As an ECKist, I knew that Soul does not enter the physical body until the first breath of life. A Catholic friend of mine advised against abortion, based upon her religious beliefs. But after much thought, I decided abortion was the best option for me. I felt comfortable with my decision.

The night before the scheduled appointment, how-ever, my decision changed. In the dream state, the Soul that would inhabit the body of my unborn child came to me. She explained that if I carried the child to term, the

183

karma that we had together would be worked off. I awoke knowing I would not be aborting this fetus.

I dropped out of college and returned home to face my next difficult decision. Would I raise the child myself or put it up for adoption?

Questions bombarded me for months. Was I ready for the responsibility of raising a child on my own? If I gave the child up for adoption, how could I be sure I'd done the right thing? Was this child truly in the hands of the Mahanta?

During this time, I became aware of the Soul that would soon be my child. I began to feel her presence strongly during my ECK Spiritual Exercises. It was soothing and comforting. As I grew to know her, I felt everything would be fine. Finally, I decided the best thing for both of us would be to put the baby up for adoption. I found an adoption agency and began the process.

According to the adoption agreement, I could name the child. But the adoptive parents could choose whether to keep the name or change it. I had no trouble picking out a boy's name, but couldn't decide on a name for a girl. This was distressing to me, because I was convinced the child would be female.

I still hadn't chosen a girl's name as the nurses wheeled me into the delivery room. But at the moment of birth, I inwardly heard the name *Elizabeth*. And it was a girl!

During my stay in the hospital, I spent as much time with Elizabeth as I could. We had three full days together. I returned her to the nursery only at night, so I could rest.

When the time came for me to check out of the hospital, our impending separation became a reality. Elizabeth would not be leaving the hospital with me!

She would be placed temporarily in a foster home until the court approved her adoption. I realized the beautiful Soul I had come to love so dearly was moving on. Pain swept through me, wrenching my emotional body as I sobbed uncontrollably. Inwardly I sang HU, a love song to God, trying to calm myself.

Then I felt Elizabeth's presence, as if she were physically in my arms. Though her physical body rested in the nursery, I heard her breathing and felt her weight. Through the love of Spirit, I knew whenever I needed Elizabeth to ease the pain of separation, somehow she would be there.

In the months following the adoption, Elizabeth came to me almost nightly during my spiritual exercises. One night, I told Divine Spirit and Elizabeth that my heart had healed enough to let her go.

I had met Elizabeth's new parents the day they came to pick her up. They were a loving couple who had waited seven years for the opportunity to adopt a child. They expressed their gratitude to me. Though they would have been happy with any child, I was amazed to find that their dream was to have a daughter—named Elizabeth!

I gave Elizabeth's adoptive parents an album I had put together; it included pictures, my autobiography, and an audiocassette explaining to Elizabeth why I chose adoption. At the end of the tape recording I sang her the song, "What I Did for Love," from the musical *A Chorus Line*. Her new parents received these gifts with open, grateful hearts.

In the adoption agreement, her parents agreed to send a report and pictures of Elizabeth every three months for the first year. Christmas arrived at the end of the first three months.

Elizabeth's mother wanted to send a Christmas gift with the report. She discussed the idea with a friend who was also an adoptive mother. The friend told her that sending a gift would only hurt my feelings. Elizabeth's mother didn't think it would hurt me, but she began to wonder.

Despite her misgivings, Elizabeth's mother decided to go shopping for an appropriate gift. The mall teemed with shoppers as she searched from store to store.

As she entered a jewelry shop, a pair of matching, heart-shaped lockets caught her glance. Perfect, she thought, one for Debby, and one for Elizabeth. Just as she was about to ask the clerk to wrap them, she recalled her friend's warnings. Since she didn't want to hurt me, she turned to leave the store.

But as she stepped from the jewelry shop, the Christmas music that had been playing over the mall loudspeaker suddenly stopped. Out came the song, "What I Did for Love." In the report she sent, she wrote, "At that moment, there was only you, me, and Elizabeth." Elizabeth's mother knew that this was God's way of reaffirming the gift. She turned around and bought the lockets.

This was also Divine Spirit's way of telling me that my decision to give Elizabeth up was right for both of us as Soul. Since then, there has never been the slightest doubt in my mind that Elizabeth truly is in the hands of the Mahanta.

7
Solving Problems
with Spirit

The Mahanta guides us through our spiritual tests.

Why Do We Have Bad Experiences?

Patti Simpson Rivinus

The October 1983 issue of *The ECK Mata Journal* carried a story by Ann Archer of her experiences in a near-fatal automobile accident.

As I read that intense drama, my skin bristled with goose bumps, the reaction which I, as Soul, use to signal the rest of my conscious being that I have been touched deeply, that someone has just spoken in my native language, the language of Soul.

By the end of Ann's tale, I found tears streaming down my face, yet I was neither sad nor happy. Like the goose bumps, the tears were also the physical entity's feeble reflection of Soul's profound response.

All I could say afterward was, "What a beautiful experience! What a beautiful and wise Soul to have had it!" And yet, to the ordinary man on the street, this would have seemed a "bad" experience. Indeed, one reader took umbrage at the whole business, asking where was Ann's spiritual master? Why had he not prevented the accident? Surely, it proved her master was not a true one.

Actually the reader missed the point entirely, as do many who think that the proof of the true path and the true master is measured by how trouble-free and euphoric one is in life.

The happy, carefree, untroubled, easy existence is not a sign that one has done everything right; it's a sign someone is resting. We may do this for a day, a week, a year, or an entire incarnation, but as Paul Twitchell, the modern-day founder of Eckankar, used to say to those of us who worked closely with him, "All growth is in the hassle."

Some years ago, I led a six-month spiritual workshop for a group of Eckankar students. One factor that I worked on a great deal was how to look inside the apparently negative experience and get the lesson of it, how to make it work for you, even how to bless it. The students were asked to write periodic reports. Among other assignments, they evaluated their own growth in terms of the material we covered and also evaluated the workshop itself.

At one point a student wrote, "I simply don't understand why you keep going over how people can work with problems. Since being in Eckankar, I have never had a problem. All anyone needs to do is stay connected to the Light and Sound, put his life entirely in the hands of the Master, and he'll not have to worry about problems. They just don't happen, if you're doing it right."

Well, this presented *me* with a problem. After I overcame the obvious inference that the wrong person was teaching the study group, I had to find a way to respond. Even though I have the reputation among my friends of telling it like it is, I can be diplomatic when I need to be. This was definitely such an occasion. I replied something like this: "I am very happy to read that since you became a student of Eckankar your life has been problem-free. I find this quite amazing, and you must surely be the exception to the rule; so far you are the only student I have met who could make this claim.

"I suppose it is possible for one to navigate the entire course without encountering a single difficulty. If you are such a one, more power to you and my congratulations. However, it usually doesn't work out quite that simply for the rest of us, so please bear with us while we struggle along."

A year or so later I ran into the individual at a seminar. He asked if we could have a private talk. It turned out that there had been a sudden, unexpected divorce accompanied by a great deal of heartache and Soul-searching. One cannot under any circumstance wish adversity on one's fellow man, nor rejoice in his misfortune. Yet, I was so relieved for this person—I was almost happy—because there was such a big change in him. The person talking to me now was real. The hard edges had softened, and there was a flexibility and a measure of compassion that had been previously missing. In short, I saw incredible growth in him.

He no longer had the arrogant posture of one who is doing it "right" while everyone else misses the point. I could not be glad for the pain that he had experienced, but I was glad for the results.

We are here, on this planet, to learn; this is our training ground for the time being. Not only do we need the hassle to grow, we ourselves set up the circumstances of our hassles. The degree to which we deny this is the degree to which we have not comprehended the nature of our test.

The statement that there is really no such thing as a bad experience seems trite. It is, however, profoundly true. But there are two main exceptions to this. First, it is a bad experience if we have it and don't bother to understand why.

This is not to say that all experiences are pleasant. However, just as the unpleasant dream is more likely to capture our attention and be remembered, thus giving us the opportunity to examine its symbolism and interpret its message, so does the unpleasant life experience rivet our attention to its components, affording us the golden opportunity, if we will take it, to understand and grow.

One exercise that the previously mentioned study group did was to draw a line graph of the ten most significant events in their lives and to put these points above or below a median line, which would represent neutral. Points were drawn in in proportion to their degree of "high" or "low."

An interesting phenomenon emerged. Each one was able to recognize that the most profound changes occurred as the result of the lowest points. A good many had a very high point not long after a very low point, indicating that the low, upsetting, unpleasant event opened doors of realization and action that catapulted their consciousness into a new zone.

And now for the other kind of bad experience I said was possible. In view of all that's been said here, you can probably guess it. In my book, anyway, the all-time bad experience is to have no experience at all!

How I Quit Smoking

Henry Kiong

My marriage to the cigarette dates back to 1957. When I discovered Eckankar in 1980, I became aware that the Inner Master, the Mahanta, discouraged smoking. It interfered with the subtle guidance of the Holy Spirit and stood as proof that I loved my outer addictions more than the inner Life Force. Still I persisted in this habit.

I knew that in order to keep progressing on the path of Eckankar I had to quit smoking when I took the Second Initiation. But that was two years away! I delighted in the reprieve and kept puffing away.

But the time passed very quickly. Another year of sporadic efforts to gradually and painlessly drop my smoking habit proved futile. Giving up a twenty-five-year partnership was no easy task!

Addicted smokers will agree that a cigarette is most enjoyable immediately after a meal. One particular morning, after a hearty breakfast, I really craved a cigarette. But I had deliberately left my cigarettes at the office the evening before. The craving became acute, but I refused the easy way out: simply buying another pack. I decided to drive to my office instead, hoping that the craving would subside during the fifteen-minute journey.

Oh, how wrong I was! The craving became so intense that when I lit up, I enjoyed the cigarette as I never had before. Little did I know that the Mahanta, in his mercy, was letting me enjoy my last cigarette.

Soon after, while driving to a job site, I had a distinct impression of just one word whispered inwardly by the Mahanta: "Breathe." Oddly enough, I immediately understood the full import of that single word. I was to breathe deeply—filling my lungs with fresh air each time I craved a cigarette. I was to breathe deeply as many times as was required to drive away the craving. I subsequently discovered it took about ten breaths.

The whole process of understanding took only a split second. What I could not understand was how my normally pragmatic conscious mind could permit me to accept it without question.

The beautiful part of it all is that the method worked! I received that message nearly six years ago. From that moment not a single cigarette has touched my lips. That inner experience is all the more memorable to me because it occurred while I was wide awake and concentrating on driving. Those of you who still smoke may wish to give the Mahanta's method a try.

Letting Go of Fear

Brandi Weaver

A couple of years ago, when I was seven, my mother was very sick. We went to visit her in the hospital but couldn't stay long because the doctors said she needed rest. We only had enough time to cheer her up with a song my Uncle Dick had written.

After we ate dinner that night, I went to bed early. As I did my spiritual exercise, I went with the Living ECK Master to a Golden Wisdom Temple that looked like a castle. I told Wah Z that I was worried about my mother dying. I asked him, "Is my mother going to be all right?"

He leaned toward me and said, "Brandi, everybody has a right to live and die. I understand how you feel, but if your mother decides to go, don't be sad. Just realize she can visit you every day and you can visit her whenever you want."

The next morning my dad was told that the doctors didn't really know what was wrong with my mom. Again, I started to worry. She'd lost so much weight and was unable to eat anything. I felt my fears building inside me like a tall, tall building. I began breathing heavily and felt uneasy eating dinner that night.

Finally, I decided to do a spiritual exercise and take a walk with Wah Z. That was when he told me my mother would be OK. But even then I couldn't stop worrying about the situation. It was too big for me. I didn't know how to handle it and couldn't even talk to my father because I didn't know what to say.

Then I sat down to think about it all and suddenly felt calm. I could hear a tiny voice inside me that sounded like my mother's. I listened, and the voice grew stronger. My mother was trying to tell me she would be all right and I had nothing to fear. The color I saw around my mother was the same color I had seen glowing around Wah Z. Finally, I knew everything would be fine.

The next week, when we went to visit my mother again, the nurses asked us to wait. None of us knew what was going on because they wouldn't say anything. I thought they were taking more tests. But when my mother came out in a wheelchair dressed in her everyday clothes, we knew she was finally coming home. We all gave her big hugs and kisses, and she cried with happiness.

The Hunt for My Wedding Dress

Cindi Arnold-Davis

For months prior to my wedding, I searched frantically for the perfect wedding dress. I wanted to find something simple and quaint—and reasonably priced. No easy task.

The stores were filled with elaborately jeweled, beaded, laced, and bowed dresses with price tags to match. My requests for something more country-simple, old-fashioned, and plain only drew smiles from the well-meaning store clerks.

But I persisted. I traveled the area, combing wedding boutiques and antique stores to no avail. As the wedding date approached, I became more and more anxious.

One day I was unexpectedly given the afternoon off from work. As I headed to my car, I silently asked the Inner Master to guide me in my search for the right wedding dress.

I started driving. As I listened inwardly, gentle nudges began to lead me to a well-hidden store I'd never seen before. I got out of the car and walked to the shop. Almost immediately upon entering, I spotted—you guessed it—a white dress. Antique at that. Simple. Lovely.

But my hunt had left me pretty skeptical. The dress still had to meet a specific checklist of requirements. I didn't want to raise my hopes for nothing. So I mentally went through the list.

Yes, the fabric looks good; yes, the sewing and styling are careful and elegant. But what about the price? The question generally put an end to my potential purchase. I lifted the price tag, and my eyes opened wider. The price was indeed very reasonable.

Still not believing my find, I went to the clerk to ask if I could try the dress on. Even though no dressing room was in sight, I vowed not to buy the dress if I couldn't try it on first. Even a bargain is too expensive if it doesn't fit.

The clerk pointed to a small dressing room. After I put on the dress, I decided to wear it around the shop to see if it felt right.

As I walked around browsing, several shoppers commented on the dress. One exclaimed that the dress looked lovely; another claimed it was perfect for me. I also received two mock marriage proposals on the spot.

I was still stunned by suddenly finding the dress—only moments after asking for inner guidance. Well, I thought, if I don't get it now, someone else will snatch it up. If I do find something better, I'm not out much money. I decided to buy it.

Silently thanking the Inner Master and bubbling with happiness, I changed clothes and brought the dress up to the counter to pay for it. Nothing could top this wonderful gift, I thought. Imagine my surprise when the clerk told me all clothes were on sale that day at half price! What a beautiful and unexpected gift from the ECK.

I suppose the lessons we learn are always more obvious after we learn them. It seems so clear to me now that if I had only given up my anxiety to Spirit sooner, my dress hunt would have been simpler. Sometimes I forget how all-providing the ECK is.

Controlling Psychic Attacks

Julie Spurr

Current public interest in the psychic forces is a path which can lead to destruction and madness. I know, because it is the innocently curious like myself who are often the victims. Quite unwittingly, I became a target of a person controlled by a psychic entity.

Associations of this kind can develop through the use of hallucinogenics and other recreational drugs. They puncture holes in the human aura and allow negative forces to enter into a person. A human pawn of these forces will usually appear magnetically alluring to those who are interested in the psychic worlds.

I was living in Greece when I met one of these pawns, who appeared very attractive to me. I had just whetted my appetite for mystery with a few psychic tricks, such as guessing my friend's thoughts and knowing when the phone would ring.

Suddenly and unknowingly, I found myself ensnared in a terrifying web—a waking nightmare of confusion and unreality. The psychic attack on my emotional body (the feeling center of my inner self) had but one purpose—complete control.

Under his influence, we traveled to India. Our surroundings seemed to make little difference, because the siege originated in the Astral, or emotional, worlds. I began to realize that even if I fled a thousand miles from this man, I would feel no safer.

The attack, like all psychic invasions, was a severe violation of the spiritual laws. There is almost always an emotional tie of some kind, as I had with my attacker. It is this tie which must be broken in order to stop the nightmare and restore balance.

But I was unaware of being controlled. I harbored warm and benevolent feelings toward my destroyer. He kept me endlessly fascinated and always off-balance. My every move was anticipated, every attempt at freedom parried. All I knew was that I was unhappy and troubled.

I was more fortunate than many, because I had several friends in the States who were students of Eckankar. One knew of my interest in the psychic and had explained the power of the ECK word HU (pronounced like the man's name, Hugh), an ancient name for God.

It wasn't until I was at the point where my awareness, dim though it was, told me I would not survive much longer in the physical world, that I made the conscious decision to try to save myself.

One night, twelve thousand miles from home on a beach in India, I went out into the backyard and chanted the word HU.

The effect was almost instantaneous. First, my traveling companion responded with a vicious psychic attack; then, unexpectedly, he became lucid and admitted he had made a pact with an entity under whose control he operated.

He released me to stay or leave as I saw fit, adding that he was only temporarily able to offer me this choice. Chanting HU had loosed his psychic web.

I immediately packed my bag in the predawn twilight and within twenty-four hours was on a plane back to the United States. The tie was broken.

But I knew I was still far from being out of danger. I felt mildly hysterical, mentally and emotionally bruised, and certainly very confused. I now had firsthand knowledge of the psychic worlds and was desperate to find someone who could explain what had occurred.

I called a good friend and got instead the ECKist who had told me of the HU. He knew immediately that I needed help and said, "Do you want me to come over?" I answered, "Yes."

When he arrived, the first question the ECKist asked was, "Do you want to break off all ties with the psychic?" It was my sole responsibility to make the choice, allowing help and protection to flood to my aid.

I asked for the protection of the Living ECK Master, and we began a spiritual exercise using what he called the mirror technique. I imagined my whole body to be a shiny mirror reflecting away from me.

According to my friend, psychic power was all attack—it had no defense. The mirror simply returned everything to the attacker.

I pestered the ECKist with questions; to my great frustration he merely smiled and said (with what I now realize was great wisdom), "I can only give you the tools. You must cut your own way through the forest!"

This was my introduction, over ten years ago, to the path of Eckankar. I immediately began studying the ECK discourses which gave me hundreds of other spiritual techniques—but this first gift made all else possible.

We Are Soul

Constance Chang

My husband and I went to a stage show which featured a well-known hypnotist. What attracted us was the advertising phrase: You will be laughing hilariously! We always enjoy a good laugh, and true to the promise, we laughed from beginning to end.

It was only when I spoke to one of the participants after the show that I recognized an important spiritual lesson. The lesson was: Although everything in the lower worlds is illusion, we can avoid being made puppets of the Kal Niranjan, the negative power that rules the lower worlds.

I will give a few examples to illustrate the point:

When the entertainer asked for volunteers from the audience, about thirty people rushed to the stage to participate. The hypnotist seemed able to identify those whose minds would easily succumb to suggestions. The rest of the volunteers were politely asked to step down.

About twenty people remained on stage; they sat in a row facing the audience. The entertainer explained they would all be actors and actresses for the night. Those twenty people allowed the hypnotist to control them just as we allow illusion to control us.

The hypnotist said that when he counted to three, all of them would fall into a deep sleep. He told them that sometimes a specific instruction would apply only to a single person, otherwise the instruction given would be for everyone on stage. One by one, he made them perform.

Case Number One

He spoke to a young man and told him to listen while he played a piece of music from a tape. He told the man that whenever that music played, he had to get out of his seat and start conducting an orchestra.

Throughout the two-hour show, whenever this piece of music was played, the man would stand up to conduct an invisible orchestra.

Case Number Two

He selected another man and played him a marching tune. "Whenever you hear that tune," he commanded, "you must stand up and march." Obediently, the man stood up to march whenever he heard this tune.

Case Number Three

He told all twenty participants that when they heard the song, "I'm in the Mood for Love," they must kiss and hug the person nearest to them.

Each time this music was played, each and every participant stood up to kiss and hug the person nearest to him. When the music stopped, they wondered why they where hugging a stranger.

Case Number Four

The hypnotist spoke to a large middle-aged lady. He asked her to count her fingers, from one to ten, but to skip the number seven. She put up her ten fingers and began counting one to ten, leaving out seven without realizing it. She did it again and again, and found, each time, that she had eleven fingers. This made her very worried. She quietly counted her fingers over and over again for the rest of the evening.

* * *

The participants had subjected themselves to the entertainer's control throughout the evening. After the show, I had the opportunity to speak to one of the participants. When he was released from the hypnotic state, he thought he had only been on stage for six or seven minutes. He said he would never agree to participate in that manner again. He had gone up on stage thinking he could not be hypnotized.

The show demonstrated how easily we can succumb to the Kal, the negative power, without even realizing it. If we are not aware of the Kal's influence and do not have a strong mind to keep illusion at bay, we can end up like those participants—puppets and slaves to whatever illusion we find ourselves in. If we challenge illusion by saying we cannot fall into its trap, life takes up the challenge—and gives our minds suggestions.

Everything in the lower worlds is illusory. The participants saw what the entertainer wanted them to see, heard what he wanted them to hear, and did what he wanted them to do. To them, all that they saw, heard, and did was real.

If we practice the presence of the Mahanta and do the daily Spiritual Exercises of Eckankar, it helps us resist the pressures of society and the Kal's subtle suggestions. Otherwise we can be completely unaware of being controlled by illusion, just like those participants who obeyed every command of the entertainer.

My husband and I went to the show for a good laugh but ended up realizing we could be unwitting puppets of the Kal if we are not alert in our daily life.

The spiritual seeker must strive to become constantly aware of his true divinity as Soul. Soul is here to gain experience in the lower worlds of illusion. Eventually we learn how to see through the tricks of the Kal Niranjan and return to the Godhead, to serve as a divine Co-worker with God. This is our spiritual mission in life.

Journey through Cotonou

Ulrico Sacchet

The rooster's crow called me back from my dreams. Slowly I gathered myself. The warm tropical ocean air wafted through the open window, filling the dawning day with excitement. Sitting up on the comfortably hard mat, a shadow tried to enter my mind.

Today was January 15, 1977, my fifth day in Togo, Africa, where my visa only authorized a visit of four days. But I swept it aside for now. Before anything else I was to do my spiritual exercise, by softly chanting my holy word and bathing myself in the Light and Sound of God. I knew this would align me with Spirit, increase awareness of my inner guidance, and thus carry me smoothly through the day, even this one!

The midday sun was burning hot on the lovely city of Lomé as I made my way to the beachside market-place. I wanted to find a ride to nearby Benin, the next country on my schedule. The morning had passed quickly with deliciously ripe pineapple at a friend's home and a brief visit to a mango plantation. How easy it would have been to extend my visa, to stay a little longer in that beautiful place.

209

But as I looked within, listening to that inner voice, it came across gently but very clearly: "There is a reason why the visa expires after only four days. You had better go with the flow of events!" And so I did, for I had learned to trust my inner guidance, the individual inner experience with the Light and Sound of ECK, the communication with the Inner Master. I have found it is the only real thing we can safely base our lives upon.

I was sitting on a bench in the shade of the customs hut of D'Illa-Condji, waiting for the officers inside to inspect my passport and transit-visa and give me permission to enter Benin. The other ten or twelve passengers of that station-wagon shuttle were already cleared, busy piling their bags and bundles back on top of the car. Even a cage with noisy chickens was back on the car roof. The driver started gathering his passengers, for the vehicles in front had moved on, and the ones behind started preparing to leave too.

Finally I was called in. Two officers, with my passport in front of them, greeted me with a cold glance across the gray table. I was not allowed to enter Benin: they denied me permission to go ahead! But I had a valid entry visa to cross through to Nigeria where my mail was waiting for me in Lagos. I would not consider turning back. We haggled back and forth, neither side willing to give in. I was confused about the turn of events. There was no question within me; I was to go forward! Even if I had wanted, the Togolese would not let me back in; that visa had expired. But then I remembered: "You had better go with the flow!"

I let go. There was nothing to haggle about, but neither was there any place to go. So I sat there in the bare, gray room with the somber officers and wondered what would come next. The people outside started to get impatient. The shuttle was blocking the road. Shouting and honking filled the air. The driver's face appeared in the door. They talked in Ewe, their native tongue. I felt lost, a stranger stuck between two strange lands. There was just one thing left to do.

Silently I started chanting HU, the ancient name of God, asking the Living ECK Master for help and handing the situation over to Spirit. Sure enough, a stamp suddenly clashed onto my passport and something was written by hand, "transit direct sans arrêt au Benin." I was to go directly to Nigeria, without stopping in Benin. My passport was given to the driver, who grabbed my arm, and off we went.

I was squeezed in between two huge native ladies with little babies and big bags, and the shuttle took off. With my passport in the driver's pocket I felt rather uneasy, a little like a prisoner, but I was happy to finally be moving ahead. After all, I should appreciate the assistance of the driver. He was actually heading all the way to the Nigerian border and not just to Cotonou, as he was originally paid to do.

The scenery was some of the most beautiful I have ever seen: the setting sun, the ocean. Tall palm trees stretched for miles along the balmy beach, caressed by a gentle, warm breeze filled with sweet perfumes. The car had become less crowded after a stop in Cotonou, where most passengers had disembarked. The driver was watching me closely, and I wondered how this all would end.

It was almost midnight. Torn out of my slumber, I saw my passport change hands to an officer standing outside in the dark. The driver helped me get my bag from the roof, turned around, and was gone. Handing me the passport, the officer pointed to a light in the distance. We had reached Igolo, on the other side of

Benin. The light was the Nigerian border, Idiroko. Sighing with relief, I shouldered my bag to walk toward the light, tired and curious about what would await me there.

The Nigerian officer laughed at me, stamping my passport for twice as long a stay as my visa entitled me to stay.

It was about one or two o'clock in the morning when I went my way, humming a melody of gratefulness to Spirit. It was not till months later, back in Europe, that I began to realize the depth of that experience and the divine protection and guidance I had received that day.

I never cared to find out exactly what happened that night in Benin, but I heard of upheaval, revolution, and white people being shot dead in the streets of Cotonou. The country's borders were totally closed to any traffic or mail for many months. I had missed it by just a few hours. How easy it is to overlook the depth of the guidance and protection we receive from Spirit, from the ECK; yet It is with us all the way!

8

Making Dreams Come True

Touching the Spirit of God brings our dreams to life.

Dream, and It Might Come True

Peggy McCardle

This is the third year I've had my perfect job. It's the most interesting and rewarding job I've ever had, because I asked Spirit to help me dream it up!

Four years ago, I lived in the southern United States. The work I did was interesting. I taught speech-language pathology at a university, and I was fairly successful at it. Life was good. I liked the climate and the folks I worked with. And I was becoming a serious jogger; every day I rose at dawn and ran four to five miles.

One weekend at the beginning of the fall semester, I decided to enter a ten-kilometer race with some friends. As I got out of the car and jogged over to the table to pick up my racing number, I tripped over a speed bump in the parking lot. A simple little fall. I can still see it all in slow motion.

As I tripped and went down, a pinpoint of pain started in my heel, shot like lightning up my right leg, and exploded in my hip. Suddenly on the ground with tears in my eyes, I smiled and said to myself, Karma! I must have done something really bad this time! I don't

215

remember it hurting much—but I do recall wondering why I had fallen. I watched my girlfriend win third-place honors in the race and then rode home in the back of the station wagon, sleeping with the help of some aspirin. I couldn't put any weight on my leg.

A few X rays later, I discovered the simple little fall had fractured my hip socket! The doctor made me an offer: traction in the hospital for six weeks or traction at home for six weeks. I chose home. With the help of my colleagues, I kept up my work. I taught classes from a single bed in the middle of my living room. Every day, I practiced the Spiritual Exercises of ECK, which helped me control the pain. I didn't need any medication after those first few aspirin I took the day I fell.

I had a lot of time to look within and think. My husband's job was ending in six months. We knew one of us had to find a job in a city where the other could also find work. Our small town had nothing further to offer my husband in his chosen profession, and I realized I wanted to move back to the East Coast, where my family lived.

I began to play a game with the ECK—like deciding how you'd spend a million dollars if you won a sweepstakes. This game was called "My Perfect Job." I asked the Inner Master, Wah Z: What if I could design my own perfect job? What would it look and feel like?

Over the next several weeks, I decided my ideal job would be in a large metropolitan hospital, where I'd diagnose children's speech problems. The hospital would also have a medical-school affiliation so I could do research. I knew as I dreamed that such a job didn't exist—or if it did, I didn't know where! But it was such a fun game to play. Over and over again, I focused on the image of my ideal job, releasing it to the ECK each time.

216

As soon as I was up and around on crutches, life got busy and hectic again. I forgot about my game. I did send out a few job inquiries and even applied to a hospital in the Washington, D.C., area.

A few weeks later, I got a notice in the mail describing a job at a large medical center. As I called the hospital, I had a sinking feeling that the job would involve adult patients, because it was a military medical center. Imagine my surprise when the personnel director said, "I don't even have a job description to read you yet. It's a brand-new position in pediatrics though, working with children. I wish I could tell you more about what the job will entail," she finished lamely.

Inside, I shouted, "Maybe you can't, but I can. Because this is my dream job!" The next week, I flew there, interviewed, and got the job. It had everything I wanted—and lots of things I hadn't even thought to ask for. That's the way Spirit works, when you dream with detachment.

I guess folks get tired of hearing the old clichés, such as: "everything happens for a reason," or "look for the silver lining." But when things get rough I remind myself: I got the best job I ever had as a result of what everyone thought was the worst thing that ever happened to me! I've learned to relax in the arms of Spirit—and dream with love and a light heart.

Getting Practical Spiritual Guidance

Ann Rafferty

In the Company of ECK Masters. "Hmmm, catchy title." My friend had loaned me a copy of this book by Phil Morimitsu. She'd described the book in glowing terms, and I'd asked to borrow it. It was an account of a chela's experiences with the teachings of Eckankar.

As I read about the author's inner conversations with the ECK Masters and ancient followers of ECK, my mind rebelled. "Is this guy for real?" it sneered. I was jealous; I had no recollection of being instructed by ECK Masters during my thirteen years as a member of Eckankar.

But as the short chapters flew by, these reactions calmed. Quietly, at first, I began to sense inner words that were being spoken to me. Instead of actually hearing them, the words gently bubbled up within me. I recognized the voice of the Living ECK Master, Sri Harold Klemp, who as the Inner Master is also known as Wah Z.

"All you have to do is ask, Ann, and be open to the gifts of Spirit. Experiences will come, to the degree you surrender to the ECK and my love for you. Know that

Spirit works in whatever way necessary to instruct and reach Soul. An attitude of gratitude and love will help you see yourself as Soul."

Right then and there, I made a conscious agreement with the ECK. I would listen closely and follow Its guidance, no matter how subtle. Each night I would record the small incidents of the day, looking for spiritual parables and lessons.

Shortly after making this agreement, Spirit obliged me with an inner experience. I was driving to work and feeling annoyed. I was going to be late. But instead of getting angry, I said aloud, "OK, I'm going to surrender all this irritation to Spirit and see what lessons are here for me."

Cautiously, I glanced at the passenger's seat, to see if Wah Z, the Inner Master, had appeared. "OK. So I don't see you in the physical like others do. I still know you're with me every second, showering me with love and guidance." I felt a blanket of love surround me in response.

A few yards down the road, it started to rain. I flicked on the wipers, but nothing happened. I remembered that a few days ago, a fuse had blown in my car. My husband had borrowed the fuse for the wipers to fix it! Shaking my head and rolling my eyes toward the heavens, I chuckled, "I give up." I was surrendering to Spirit, rather than to anger. It sure would have been easy to start mentally blaming my husband for being careless.

As I struggled to see through the rain, I once again became aware of words bubbling into my consciousness: Driving without your wipers on a rainy day is like going through life without being aware of the love and guidance of the Mahanta. It's possible, but the way is much slower and more dangerous—not to mention anxious! When you surrender to the guidance of the Mahanta, your inner wipers are on and working. You're able to travel with clear vision in a relaxed fashion.

I felt a deep gratitude as I pulled into my parking space at work. I had arrived safely—and recognized a spiritual lesson right under my nose! The subtlety of it amazed me, and I wondered how many lessons I'd missed. But I felt no regret. For I now know what my inner voice sounds like!

Since that time my husband and I have started swapping tales about the inner voice. They happen each day. We learn from each other. These stories also provide a comfortable way to introduce someone to the Eckankar teachings. Everyone can grasp a natural example of how Spirit guides us. We only have to surrender, listen, and trust the ECK.

Making Your Dreams Come True

Dian Deutsch

I can still recall asking my father, when I was quite young, if there were any parts of the world that had not yet been discovered. Although I was disappointed to learn that all the world had indeed been named, mapped, and conquered, I did not lose heart. I decided to be an explorer anyway, to make the world new through my own eyes and experience.

Since forming that early conviction and later becoming an ECKist, I have become a true explorer in both the inner and outer worlds. In this world, I have traveled through Europe several times, lived in France and Ireland, and soon hope to teach English in the Far East. As with all experiences in life, traveling has taught me many lessons. I have learned that dreams can become a reality through the power of imagination and commitment to one's goals. Also, once a dream comes true, it's important not to be attached to the images and expectations that brought you there.

I once traveled with a friend who was unable, or at least unwilling, to make this transition. She was so attached to her ideals that she was disappointed when she actually realized her dream—in this case, visiting Europe. She spent the holiday complaining, criticizing the countries we visited, and constantly comparing everything to her dream, which, by now, should have been discarded like a worn-out tool.

There was such tension between her expectations and her experience that she finally had to make a choice between the two—and went home early. In contrast, I accepted that my dreams were valid; in fact, they were my true passport. But I also knew that my dreams were just the beginning. The dreams and expectations were a framework that had to fall away to allow the living creation—the here and now—to occur.

The above story, of course, has to do with attitude. A positive, open attitude, like a sense of humor, is an everyday survival factor, no matter where you are. But when traveling, when experiences seem to hit all the harder and faster, a positive attitude is crucial. Time and time again, I have seen that the kind of day I have has less to do with externals—being shortchanged by a street vendor or missing the only boat for a week—than with how I see and react to these situations.

This law is so exact, it runs like clockwork. If I'm in a bad mood, I attract like-minded people and have a rotten day. If I remain the bright-eyed optimist, trusting Spirit for my well-being, then miracles can happen. The ECK Masters teach that miracles occur constantly. But we often simply take Spirit's presence for granted in our lives or are too busy with our "important" things to notice. Having seen just how wrong things can go when traveling, I've learned that when they go right, it's no coincidence. It's because I've let Spirit be my tour guide, right down to which train stop to get off at and which way to go to the youth hostel: up this street or up the next?

Last summer, when I was attending a traditional-music school in Ireland, I once saw the difference that trusting Spirit and the Inner Master can make. I was camping to save money and had arranged well in advance to borrow a tent from a friend. In the end however, I was unable to locate this friend (or his tent) and so had to buy an inexpensive tent at the last minute.

Before buying it, I asked the salesman several times if it was intact and included all the necessary pieces (as it was slightly used). He assured me it was fine and showed me a tent on display in the store. I didn't have time to check out the tent before leaving, but I left for my trip confident that the salesman's promises were good.

It wasn't until I was trying to set up the tent in the pouring rain that I realized it was useless. Not only was it not the tent I'd been shown in the store, but the poles were all the wrong size. There was no way this tent would stay up. I was already soaked to the bone, and every bed-and-breakfast lodging for miles around was booked (even if I could have afforded to stay in one). Since I was way out in the country, there were no camping supply stores where I could replace the poles or rent or buy another tent. What could be worse?

Tired, frustrated, and angry, I was ready to pack it all up and head back to Dublin. But instead, I consciously gave the whole situation over to the ECK, or Spirit. "There's no point in worrying about it," I decided aloud. "It's in the Mahanta's hands now, and he'll take care of it."

Feeling much better, I went for some hot soup at the makeshift restaurant set up for the school. After purchasing my meal, I sat down alone at a table. Almost immediately a woman came over and asked if she could join me. "I won't be much company," I warned, "but be my guest."

"Why?" she asked.

I hesitated. "Do you really want to know?" At her insistence, I proceeded to tell my tale.

As she listened, the woman grew happier and happier. When I'd finished she exclaimed. "That's no problem! I've a brand-new four-man tent already set up, and I don't like camping alone. You can stay the whole week with me for free."

This dry tent was one gift from Spirit I did not take for granted. Many times during the week I thanked the Mahanta as I not only enjoyed the tent but also the company of a new friend.

Trusting Spirit, of course, takes practice. It's not easy—especially at first, when you're in the habit of allowing the know-it-all mind to dictate the itinerary for both your travel and your whole life.

I can easily imagine what my week would have been like that summer in Ireland if I'd remained attached to the situation and trusted my logical reason and the little self, or ego, rather than the greater awareness of the ECK. Simply, I've learned to trust Spirit on the roads of life because I've seen what happens when I don't. More important, I've seen what little, yet amazing, miracles happen when I do.

It's Amazing What an Open Heart Can Do

Garrick Colwell

In a vivid dream, I saw the president of my company seated at his grand piano. As he played, he told me we would soon reach a parting of the ways. Sure enough, about six weeks later, we negotiated a termination contract. I would receive six months pay after I left. Spirit was providing financial stability so I could reevaluate my life both personally and professionally.

During the preceding year, a divorce had separated me from my daughter by two thousand miles—and left me with a broken heart.

The loss of my job, the divorce, and my daughter's absence brought me to a spiritual turning point. I could allow heartbreak and disappointment to paralyze me—or I could surrender to the Inner Master, the Mahanta, and open my heart to infinite possibilities.

In ECK, we learn that Divine Spirit will give us all we need. First, we must expect the best in life and be willing to work for it. Second, we develop a clear inner picture of what is needed.

I realized Spirit was providing me with an opportunity to transform my life—and let go of certain long-held attitudes. Using the Spiritual Exercises of ECK each day, I consciously worked on the first two steps for bringing bounty into my life. The third step—opening my heart to change—came with the help of Spirit.

As I worked with the Inner Master during these daily twenty-minute contemplations, I discovered three things were important to my happiness: to be near my daughter, to find enriching employment, and to find a fulfilling relationship. I asked Spirit for someone I could love as an equal. I decided on these priorities in early June—then promptly released them as I placed my attention elsewhere.

On June 24, the day I received the final divorce papers, I met a woman named Mary. On June 28, we met again casually. We both knew something was happening between us, though we didn't do a lot about it.

I made plans to visit my daughter in Austin, Texas, in early July. On the day before I was scheduled to leave, I got a call from the president of a San Antonio-based company—an hour's drive from Austin.

The president said, "Listen, we've heard about you. We need a vice president of Sales and Marketing, and we'd like to talk to you."

"Well, that's great," I replied. "I'm planning to be in Austin tomorrow. I'll see you as soon as I can fit it into my schedule. I'll call tomorrow, and we'll go from there."

He said, "Fine, I'll talk to you then."

My Tuesday-morning flight to Austin had a three-hour layover in Phoenix. I planned to have lunch with an associate and discuss some business opportunities. Just before I left for the airport, he called to cancel our luncheon. Inwardly, I wondered why this block of time had opened up.

Once on board the plane, I mentioned to the flight crew that I was going to Austin and perhaps San Antonio, and we chatted a bit. As I was getting off the plane in Phoenix, a stewardess asked, "Aren't you going on with us to San Antonio?"

"I don't understand," I replied quizzically.

Again she said, "You *are* going to San Antonio, aren't you? Why don't you come with us? We'll be changing to another plane." With some confusion, I explained that my destination was Austin—but at the same time I realized this was a nudge from Spirit.

As I walked into the terminal, I noticed their plane at an adjacent gate was departing for San Antonio in just ten minutes. I went to the ticket counter, displayed my nonrefundable, nonexchangeable ticket, and asked the agent, "Can I use my ticket on this flight to San Antonio, rather than Austin?" She smiled and said, "Of course. No problem."

I called the president of the company that wanted to interview me, but he was out to lunch. I explained the situation to his secretary: "I have an opportunity to fly in today. If your boss can see me, great. If he can't, we can make other arrangements when I get there."

When I arrived, the president was able to rearrange his schedule. He interviewed me for five hours. At the close of the interview, he said, "I think you're right for this position." The following Friday, I was offered the job as vice president and accepted it.

When I returned from Austin, Mary and I got together. Within a week, we decided to get married. She wasn't familiar with the teachings of Eckankar, but after I read from *The ECK Wedding Ceremony* to her, she agreed to have an ECK wedding. So in less than a month after opening my heart to the inner guidance of the Mahanta I had a new job, I was moving near my daughter, and I was getting married!

I still had to sell my house and arrange for the wedding ceremony before moving to San Antonio. Once I made the decision to put the house on the market, it sold in three hours. I signed the contract for the sale at 7:00 that night, and I accepted an offer for the full price at 10:00.

Mary and I decided to have our wedding at dawn on Wednesday, July 29. The movers would come later that same day. On Monday evening, we were eating dinner with the High Initiate of Eckankar who was to perform the ceremony. As we discussed the arrangements, we both felt an inner nudge to move the wedding up a day to Tuesday morning.

So, in the middle of dinner, we got up and raced down to the local mall. We found my suit was ready a day early; the local flower shop offered to stay open a few more minutes and make up the bouquet Mary wanted. We also found a photographer to take some wedding photos.

The sunrise on Tuesday morning was the most spectacular I've ever seen. The wedding and everything about that day was perfect. We happened to be in the area on the following morning, and there was no sunrise at all, only clouds. If we hadn't listened to the inner nudge, we would have missed that beautiful sunrise for the morning of our wedding.

Through all of this, I've learned to relax and listen to the gentle, practical guidance of Spirit. Miracles are possible in my life, if I open my heart and listen to the inner direction of the Mahanta.

9
Meetings with Spiritual Adepts

Have you met these Spiritual Masters?

Who Are the Spiritual Travelers?

Joan Klemp

The spiritual travelers are agents of God, vehicles for Divine Spirit. These ECK Masters will not interfere in the sacred state of consciousness of another being without his permission. They all work in harmony with the Living ECK Master of the time to assist those Souls who are ready to awaken to their true nature and destiny.

Sri Harold Klemp is the present Living ECK Master. As a friend and guide, his spiritual purpose is to link Soul to the Light and Sound of God. The other ECK Masters assist. Those great spiritual beings include Paul Twitchell, the modern-day founder of Eckankar, as well as Rebazar Tarzs, Gopal Das, and Lai Tsi.

The sincere spiritual seeker, who in his heart asks for truth and direction, may meet a spiritual traveler years before he ever comes across the ECK teachings. One woman had such an experience with Harold Klemp six years before she came to know him as the Living ECK Master.

In August 1975 it was necessary for her to have oral

233

surgery with a general anesthetic. She remembers being with "a man with glasses, slim, slightly built." He talked with her and gave her a tremendous feeling of being loved and cared for. He told her he had to leave for a time and gave her his name. She could see some sort of timepiece as he disappeared.

"When I woke up," she said, "I remembered his name, but later all I could remember was that it ended with a 'ji'." She was in tears at the loss. Later, in talking with friends, she was told people hallucinate during or after anesthesia. Yet she *knew* she wasn't hallucinating!

Sometime after the fall of 1981 she joined Eckankar and met the Living ECK Master, Sri Harold Klemp. Remembering her earlier experience, she exclaimed: "When I saw your name, Harji,* and looked into your eyes, I *knew* it was you. Thank you for the love then."

Another young woman had an experience with her father and Gopal Das, years before she ever heard of Eckankar or the ECK Masters. When she was sixteen her father translated (died). For a time afterward he would come to visit her. On his last visit he came with someone else. At the time she thought the man was an angel. Ten years later when she first started reading about ECK, she saw a picture of Gopal Das and realized this ECK Master was the man she had seen with her father when she was sixteen.

A young teenager went to bed feeling ill one day and asked the Spiritual Traveler Harold Klemp, the Living ECK Master, for help. He felt himself being wrapped in a wonderful cloak of protection. This gave him a feeling

---

*Harji is a respectful name of affection for Sri Harold Klemp.

of happiness and joy. Then he saw Rebazar Tarzs, who gave him a drink from his cupped hands. The liquid was refreshing. It gave him a wonderful feeling through his whole physical body and made him feel relaxed and at peace. Then Rebazar took him in a blue cloud to visit a great city full of happiness and joy. They went into a room full of lights of many colors shining down on them. After walking beside an ocean where interesting creatures lived, they went back to the city, back on the cloud, and went over the Ocean of Love and Mercy.

One ECK student had an experience with the great Chinese spiritual traveler, Lai Tsi. She was sitting in contemplation doing a spiritual exercise when the ECK Master appeared to her. "He told me," she said, "that whenever things got too rough, I could call on him and he would assist me.

"I feel most fortunate to have this Master with me. For those who do not believe that Rebazar Tarzs and the Vairagi Masters exist, I just say to them, 'Believe. Be patient. They will appear when you are least expecting them!'"

Paul Twitchell, Rebazar Tarzs, Lai Tsi, Gopal Das—these great spiritual travelers are all agents of God. They work together and harmoniously with Harold Klemp, the Living ECK Master of the time, to provide the individual spiritual seeker the greater experience as Soul.

How I Found ECKANKAR

Margaret Jackson

My first knowledge of Eckankar came through a small notice in the newspaper. It caught my eye because a friend of mine had recently written and mentioned he was studying this spiritual path.

I wrote to the address in the paper and received a lovely letter explaining a little about the ancient teachings of ECK.

Later, I watched a video on Eckankar and began chanting the sacred ECK name for God, HU, privately at home. I wondered if it would bring any results.

Raised as a Christian, I had doubts as to whether I was dabbling in something I shouldn't. I could feel the truth of Eckankar but hesitated to venture from the familiarity of the Christian rituals.

Since childhood I had experienced a small blue dot of light upon the inner screen of my awareness and heard subtle sounds in my ears. But it never occurred to me that these were evidence of the Holy Spirit in my life. I had also been taken out of my body as a child to visit my dead grandmother and walk with her.

I thought everyone experienced such things.

I had not attended my church very often in the last ten years. What it offered always seemed to stop short of reaching God on a personal level.

One night, I sang HU. I prayed to God, Jesus, the Mahanta (the Inner Master spoken of in Eckankar), and anyone else who wanted to hear me! Please give me a sign, I implored silently. Which path should I take— the path of Eckankar or the path of Christianity? I then went to sleep.

Sometime later I awoke to see my whole bedroom filled with a soft, loving, golden glow.

I sat up in bed and, out of force of habit, turned on my bedside lamp. A man in a brown hooded robe stood at the foot of my bed. His eyes looked lovingly into the very soul of me, and I knew I was safe.

We spoke to each other through our minds; no outer speech was needed. The golden glow fluttered around him as he acknowledged my indecision about which path to take to spiritual awareness. Quietly he assured me that Eckankar would lead me on my own path to God-Realization. He gently reminded me to use the singing of the HU wisely and with love, and to be aware of myself as a vehicle for Divine Spirit, the ECK.

This being also communicated to me about my karma, old and new, which might lead me away from Eckankar and the Mahanta.

For about half an hour, he shared his wisdom with me. I basked in his gaze of pure love. He knew and accepted everything about me, both good and bad.

Then he smiled; his eyes twinkled and sparkled, and he was gone.

Other proof has come to me that Eckankar is the right path for me. But this was my first experience of being totally accepted. I have not seen him again, but I can still feel his gaze. Perhaps I may meet him again one day. Here is my drawing of his face from memory.

The drawing on the left is Margaret Jackson's. To the right is an Eckankar portrait of the ECK Master Fubbi Quantz, who teaches at one of the Temples of Golden Wisdom in the inner realms. Many students of ECK study with Fubbi Quantz in the dream state or through the contemplative Spiritual Exercises of Eckankar.

Brando

Stephen Najera

In 1983, I moved away from home for the first time, leaving south Texas for a city in the Midwest. There, I embarked on a search for truth. I accepted an invitation from a man named Daniel to study with a spiritual group. As the weeks went by, his classes moved from introductory mysticism into magic, and I became a promising student.

I developed a close relationship with a woman in the class named Jane. It was a relationship originally engineered and observed by Daniel, who was our spiritual master. Jane and I spent a lot of time together practicing the psychic arts. On one occasion, we were doing a past-life regression, and an experience unfolded for me.

I saw a boy and a girl standing at the base of a pyramid. It seemed as if they were at an altar, and a man was standing over them. The man had flowing blond hair and a solid, strong face. Describing him later, I said that he looked like Marlon Brando in the movie *Superman*. I could tell that he was a great man.

Jane was very curious about this man. She continued to feel his presence around her house. We decided to ask the man who he was. When we asked him, "What is your name?" there was no reply.

"Why are you here?" we then asked.

"I'm here for Steve," he said. "I have something for him, but he is not ready yet." He paused a moment and spoke again, "He will be."

I asked this man if I could call him Brando; he smiled and said that would be fine. I felt he was my friend.

After a couple of months, Brando left. His presence had been a constant reminder to me that there was far more to truth than what Daniel and Jane had been teaching me. By the time he left, I knew that my time of studying with Daniel was over.

Daniel was reluctant to let me go, and a battle ensued on the psychic planes. These people were my only friends; leaving their sphere meant giving up everything I knew. But through a year of inner struggle with Daniel, I learned that even a black magician had no power over me if I didn't surrender myself. I learned the lesson of self-responsibility.

My experience with Brando helped me keep going. His presence made me aware that a higher truth awaited me.

A year and a half later, someone suggested I investigate Eckankar. I read some of the books and was about to begin study when I decided to go to the local Eckankar Center for an introductory lecture.

Once there, I noticed the line drawings of several ECK Masters on the wall. I broke into a cold sweat as I recognized one of the drawings as Brando. I had found the answer to a two-year-old question. His name is

Gopal Das—the great ECK Master who lived in Egypt in 3000 B.C.

My Life-after-Death Experience with Lai Tsi

Jim Hawkins

The ECK Masters of the Ancient Order of the Vairagi have been with mankind since time immemorial, always ready to aid the spiritual seeker in his quest for God Consciousness. As many of us know through our inner experiences, we have been under the tutelage of these timeless sages in past lives and continue to be helped by the Vairagi Adepts even today. Over ten years ago I received my proof of life-after-death from the ECK Master Lai Tsi, guardian of the sacred teachings of the Shariyat-Ki-Sugmad at the Temple of Golden Wisdom in the spiritual city of Arhirit. The following events occurred in 1976, while I was a sergeant in the United States Marine Corps and stationed at Camp Pendleton, California.

April 1, 1976: Tonight the first of the dreams began. I should have realized the significance of today's date, since April Fools' Day is a traditional day of playing practical jokes on people. Little did I know that the joke would soon be on me. It's hard to believe, but even ten years after those dreams I still remember each one in vivid detail.

Tonight I was chased by evil men who tied me to a stake and killed me. As my body died on the ground, I was suddenly released from that physical shell. Aren't you supposed to really be dead if you die in your dreams, I remember asking myself?

A moment later, Lai Tsi appeared at my side. I recall the warmth emanating from this great being and the perfect knowledge that we had been together before. He taught me a valuable lesson on the art of dying that night, and I knew that he was merely reminding me of what Soul already knows: Death is the greatest illusion of all.

This first lesson was more real than the waking reality that I knew as a sergeant in the Marine Corps, and I recall the great disorientation I felt upon emerging from the dream state. I can still hear myself asking out loud, upon awakening, "Was that a dream or real?"

April 30, 1976: It has now been thirty days since the first dream. Every night since April 1, I have died a sometimes peaceful, sometimes violent, death; but always a death in full color and stereo. In these dreams I would find myself looking down at my lifeless physical body and feeling absolutely wonderful at the release of Soul.

In tonight's episode, I was thrown out of an airplane. As soon as my body landed on the ground, Lai Tsi appeared. He continued my education on the true meaning of life and the unlimited options we possess as Soul in reaching the SUGMAD (God). I remember slowly waking up on the morning of May 1, feeling both joy and sorrow. I knew within myself that this was the last lesson with this beloved ECK Master. It was time to put my training into practice, although I had no idea how to apply this newfound knowledge.

May 1, 1976: Today I have exactly forty-six days left until I get out of the Marine Corps. Thank God! It seemed I would never get out. I have been having trouble with my wisdom teeth, so I checked into the dental clinic and had all four removed.

May 2, 1976: Something is not quite right. I am not sure what, but—oh well, I'll find out soon enough.

May 10, 1976: Now I am sure what is wrong: the dentist botched my minor surgery. The left side of my face has a swollen lump the size of a tennis ball, and I have a green streak of color running from my neck down to my collarbone. I go to sick bay but am told there is nothing to worry about. My inner voice gently urges me to get other help, but I ignore it. After all, a military doctor wouldn't lie to me, would he?

May 12, 1976: Today is my birthday. Happy birthday to me. My sternum has now turned dangerously gangrenous. I have systemic blood poisoning but don't know it yet. I do know the doctors are giving me the runaround. This is something serious.

Previous to this experience, I would have accepted no responsibility for my illness and "let the ECK take care of it." However, this time I listened to my inner voice, which instructed me to march into the colonel's office and lift up my shirt. Now this is something I would not normally do, since it could lead to a court-martial, but I did it anyway, and my colonel almost passed out when he saw my green sternum. He personally took me down to sick bay to see a real doctor. The cyst on my face was drained, I was given an antibiotic and sent home.

1:00 p.m.: I took the antibiotics ten minutes ago but still feel terrible. I lie down on my couch to rest, and just as I am about to pass out, I hear the voice of another ECK Master, Paul Twitchell, as clear as a bell.

247

He is saying, "If you do not listen to what I say, you will die!"

3:00 p.m.: I wake up. I am dripping with sweat and get sick several times. Paul Twitchell's voice echoes in my apartment once again. "You have five minutes to get an ambulance!" he says in no uncertain terms. I laugh and sarcastically reply to the ethers about me, "Yeah, right!" I get sick again. "You now have four minutes!" This time I listened to his warning.

The rest is a blur of action: walking next door to the gas station; calling the paramedics; passing out in the driveway; regaining consciousness in the ambulance; the paramedic trying to be funny by asking, "Having a good birthday?"; being taken into the emergency room. It is now 7:00 p.m. Just as the doctor is about to see me, a man is wheeled in who has been kicked in the head by a horse. Since I am no longer considered at risk, I am taken into a side room while the doctor treats the injured man. I look up at the clock; it is 7:10 p.m. Two more minutes and I will be twenty-two years old.

7:12 p.m.: A cold numbness starts crawling up my feet. Uh-oh, I've experienced this before in my dreams. As soon as the coldness reaches my chest, I find my consciousness has shifted to the inside of my crown chakra, located at the top of my head. It is a strange sensation to look down at the interior of my body. An instant later, I find myself being pulled right out through the top of my head! The title of Paul Twitchell's biography, *In My Soul I Am Free,* takes on new meaning. I later found out I was clinically dead at that moment. Happy birthday!

Throughout his literature, Paul Twitchell describes the Soul experience in very vivid terms. All I can say is that no words do justice to the experience, as he also points out in his various books. As Soul, I was a 360-

degree viewpoint, traveling through a tunnel of light. It was incredible! I arrived at a grassy knoll, overlooking a yellow sea and felt a tremendous presence of love surround me. I remembered being taught to send out love as soon as someone crosses over the threshold of death, and as soon as I did this myself, I was surrounded by hundreds of beings, all of whom I had known in previous incarnations.

Lai Tsi emerged from this circle of great love and communicated to me, "As you know, your physical body no longer functions in your previous world. But you have a choice. You can remain here with us and continue your experiences, or you can go back to your physical body and live out the life you planned. The choice is yours."

Before I continue with this story, I must confirm that, as it is said in the Eckankar teachings, thoughts manifest instantly in the higher worlds.

As Lai Tsi and the others hovered over the grassy knoll, I clearly remember thinking, Well, I only have five weeks left in the Marine Corps.

Instantaneously, I was transported back into my physical body. The heaviness of my physical shell was immense after experiencing life as Soul, and I cursed myself thoroughly for what I had done—weighing the five more weeks in the Marines against a blissful life in heaven. After I was through cursing, however, I opened my eyes to pitch darkness, and Lai Tsi's voice said to me, "Did you think we would let you die when you had decided to live?" As his merry laughter trailed off into the ethers, I regained my vision to see a worried nurse standing over me, giving an injection. You should have seen the strange way she looked at me when I opened my eyes and started laughing!

Lai Tsi gave me an invaluable lesson about life and death, and to this day I try to live life as fully as possible. I have my proof of life after death, as taught to me by the great spiritual ECK Master Lai Tsi, and that's something no one can ever take away.

An Appearance by the Tibetan ECK Master, Rebazar Tarzs

Joyce Caryl

For nearly two years my sister Jane, who is a psychiatrist, had been going through the experience of being publicly maligned by the press. Quite by mistake her secretary had incorrectly billed a patient, and one of the large health insurance companies decided to use Jane as a legal test case. They took her to court and let her have it with both barrels.

Her lawyer extracted more and more money from her only to drop the case at the last minute. Upon investigation Jane found that her case was indeed indefensible and that he had been leading her down the proverbial garden path.

In our phone conversations (Jane lives in another state), I could hear the exhaustion and discouragement in her voice. She didn't know if she could get through a court appearance with lawyers hurling accusations at her. "Joyce, even though I'm innocent, I'm afraid I'll break down emotionally, which will make me look guilty."

That conversation prompted me to write her a letter with a message that came from deep within myself.

I told her about the dark night of Soul—a time of desolation we experience for our spiritual benefit. I explained that it was often a turning point in our lives.

"The ECK Masters are dedicated to helping Souls through this dark night of Soul. They often appear in dreams, so examine your nightly adventures closely. I am enclosing a copy of the *ECKANKAR Journal*—be sure to read the article by Sri Harold Klemp in which he recommends softly singing 'HU—Mahanta' for spiritual help."

The next time I talked to Jane, she had been through her first court appearance. She mentioned that she had repeated that phrase, "HU—Mahanta," over and over to herself. It seemed to keep her mind off the negative situation. I said I was glad to hear that and asked if she could she remember any helpful dreams.

"Well, it's funny. I can't seem to remember my dreams, but my friends have gone out of their way to tell me theirs. And people have been helpful. I especially remember this unusual priest. I first noticed him looking at me in the courtroom. Later, when I went downstairs to fill out some papers, he was there, too. He came over and put his hand on my shoulder and said, 'I know the trouble you are going through. It will turn out for the best.' How would he know that, since I've never seen him before?"

At that point it occurred to me to ask what this priest looked like. She gave me an exact description of the great Tibetan ECK Master, Rebazar Tarzs! I suggested that perhaps he was one of the ECK Masters of the Order of Vairagi that I had told her about.

Some weeks went by before we talked again, at which time she said, "Joyce, it's the most amazing thing! I was looking through the *ECKANKAR Journal*, and there was a picture of the priest. His name is Rebazar Tarzs!"

The postscript to this story is that Jane's trouble wasn't alleviated. She had to endure the accusations made in court and upheld by the law, and so lost her means of livelihood in that state. The strain was too much for her marriage, and it fell apart. But the last time I spoke to my sister she seemed rejuvenated. She was very excited about starting her new life on Cape Cod, which, she said, is like a dream come true. And I know I'll write her a letter from time to time from that place deep within, so we can both learn more about the mysterious ways of Spirit.

Thirty Years Becoming an ECKist

Joseph Hunter

Before 1982, I'd never heard the name Eckankar. In October of that year, I met a young lady while visiting my sisters in Gary, Indiana. She told me she was an ECKist.

My reply: "What's an ECKist?"

Well, she told me. So when I got back home to Dayton, Ohio, I picked up some materials on Eckankar. That's when it came back to me.

Thirty years before, I had met a man I could never forget. When I turned to a picture of Rebazar Tarzs in the ECK material, I said, "That's him!"

*   *   *

I was driving my cab on the night shift in Milwaukee. A call came over the radio, and I said to myself, "I want that call!" But I was six or eight miles away and figured I'd never make it in time. Still, I started driving in that direction.

Thirty-five minutes passed and still no one took the call, so the dispatcher gave it to me as soon as I came in. I will never forget the man I picked up.

I drove up to the curb, got out, opened the back door, and asked the man to get in. "No thanks," he said, "I'll sit in the front with you." When I glanced up into his eyes, they seemed to look right through me.

We started out for our destination, the North Shore Station. As we drove, he sat there and told me everything about myself, even my secret prayers—things that no human being alive could know. I felt like someone had poured hot water over me.

Before stepping out of the cab, he turned and said, "We will meet again." This was Rebazar Tarzs.

A few weeks later, a friend and I had to make a rush trip to Toledo, Ohio, through pouring rain. I was driving at speeds up to a hundred miles an hour.

Just outside the suburbs of Milwaukee, a traffic light flashed red, and I was forced to stop. Suddenly the car felt funny, and when the signal changed, it wouldn't steer!

My friend and I gave a groan and climbed out into the rain to investigate. Once glance told the story. The front wheels were sagging in different directions, totally out of control. The tie-rod had come loose.

We stood quietly for a moment, thinking about what could have happened if the rod had fallen off five minutes earlier. There would've been no way to steer!

Before we could say anything, another driver got out to ask if he could help. I explained the situation and said there was really nothing he could do. The man didn't say anything before walking back to his car, so we assumed he was leaving.

But after a moment the fellow returned, and we just stood there as he knelt beside the helpless car. After a few minutes, the man straightened up and said, "It's OK now!"

Naturally, we both bent down to look at the tie-rod as he jumped into his car and sped away. It was fixed! Shock and amazement hit both of us at the same time, and we turned to each other, saying, "Are you thinking what I'm thinking?"

We drove the rest of the trip in silence. I kept muttering to myself that I couldn't wait to get home, get down on my knees, and thank God for saving my life. I felt that was the only way I had been spared.

As soon as I got home, I made good on my promise. I marched upstairs to my room, shut the door, and got down to pray. I remember saying I wanted to thank Him for saving my life and that I wanted proof that He heard me.

Well, I got my proof. While on my knees, It, the Spirit of God, took me out of my body. No words can describe all the things that happened in that room. When I got back into my body, I was hollering, "I believe, and I'll never doubt again!"

Then a voice chuckled, "I told you we would meet again!"

Many times after that, that inner voice helped me through difficult situations, letting me know, "I am always with you." Again, this was Rebazar Tarzs.

* * *

Thirty years later, after recognizing the picture of Rebazar Tarzs in the Eckankar material, I had another experience I'd like to share.

My car was hit while it was parked one night. I didn't even notice the damage till the next day, when I parked in the same spot.

So I went down to the police station and made out all the routine reports. As I walked back to my car, someone pulled into the police parking lot and parked next to a truck. Darned if the inner voice didn't speak up and say, "That truck hit your car."

So I turned around (I was through doubting this time!), went back in, and told the sergeant. Naturally he exclaimed, "How would you know?"

"Well," I replied, "just check it out." So he did, and sure enough, it was the truck.

Now you know why—after thirty years of miracles—I know ECK is for me!

A Visit from a Master

Paul Schoolcraft

Long ago in Syracuse, New York, I became friends with a man who once had a mysterious encounter with the founder of Eckankar, Paul Twitchell. One night while I was visiting my friend's home in that city, he asked if he could tell me a story. He said it was the only miracle that he was certain of in this life.

As he started his narrative in a low voice, I leaned toward him. His eyes were shining as he said, "This is exactly what I remember about that day ten years ago." His sincerity struck me deeply.

Sometime in 1969, my friend, who I'll call John, came upon a book about the life and times of Paul Twitchell. His curiosity piqued by the title, he purchased and read *In My Soul I Am Free;* it left a lasting impression upon him.

Several years passed in which John suffered greatly from heart trouble. Poor health eventually forced him to lighten his work load, and he took a job as a security guard in an office building in Syracuse.

259

The fascinating story of Paul Twitchell was often in John's thoughts, and he didn't know how to quench his burning interest in the spiritual Master.

Finally, in February 1974, he sat down and wrote Paul a letter in care of Eckankar. He humbly asked for assistance with his heart condition, and for more information about the Ancient Science of Soul Travel. He also ordered *The Flute of God,* another book by Paul.

Shortly after 4:00 p.m. on February 22, 1974, John was at work as usual with his partner, when a man entered the building and approached the two security guards.

The stranger was dressed in light blue shirt and pants. John had noticed the man immediately as he came into the busy lobby, for he wore only a light jacket. His attire would not normally be considered adequate for Syracuse's cold winters. As John watched him, the man walked straight over to ask where the phones were.

Then touching both the guards' hands as if on impulse, the stranger inquired if they had ever received an Irish blessing.

At this point in the story, John digressed to explain that he had always been interested in anything Irish, whether an Irish joke or song, though he was not of Irish ancestry.

With a smile, my friend got up to stoke the fire in his cozy living room, and continued his tale.

"The stranger in front of my partner and me began this Irish blessing, but we couldn't understand a word he said. I don't know what language he was speaking. Anyway, there was an intensity about this fellow that was not ordinary; he radiated warmth and love as he spoke."

Visibly moved, John stopped his narrative to take a deep breath. "After he finished the Irish blessing, the man in blue stepped closer and pressed his hand against my chest—directly over the heart. Time seemed to stop for a moment. Then he asked a second time where the telephones were, as if nothing unusual had taken place. But he left the building without going near a phone."

John and his partner never moved a muscle throughout this unique episode. They were caught up in the strangeness of the fleeting moment and the person who had created it.

The very next day, John's copy of the *The Flute of God* arrived in the mail. Looking at the back cover, he was astonished. The author looked exactly like the lobby visitor who had acted so strangely the day before!

During that weekend, my friend wrestled with the implications of the stranger's visit. His health condition had vanished; the rhythm of his heartbeat was strong and steady for the first time in years. After reading *The Flute of God* from cover to cover, John slipped it into his jacket to show his partner on Monday.

As soon as he got to work, he pulled out the book and again scrutinized the cover. Then he handed it to his co-worker, asking casually, "Ever seen that guy before?"

"Sure," replied his partner, "That's the fellow who was in here Friday afternoon. Who is he, anyway?"

John just shook his head and smiled. Paul Twitchell's life in the physical form had ended almost two and a half years earlier, on September 17, 1971.

A Meeting with Rebazar Tarzs

Dan Stryder

Rebazar Tarzs is a Tibetan ECK Master who has been the spiritual teacher of many Living ECK Masters, including Paul Twitchell, to whom he passed the Rod of ECK Power in 1965. Said to be over five hundred years old, Rebazar Tarzs lives in a hut in the Hindu Kush Mountains and appears to many people as he helps the present Living ECK Master, Sri Harold Klemp, in the works of Eckankar.

Suddenly, the Tibetan ECK Master, Rebazar Tarzs, was standing before me in the dim alley where I walked. His gaze was intense.

"Do you understand what the Living ECK Master was trying to show you with your last experience?" he said abruptly. "I don't think you do!"

The sudden appearance of this maroon-robed Adept sparked a deep emotion in me, for he had been in my thoughts constantly all day. For some reason, the sound of his voice and image of his face had been just beneath the surface of my thinking, as if about to emerge. Now here he was, his black hair and beard fading into the dark shadows of the twilight, a peaceful glint in his eyes.

"Do you mean the Soul Travel experience last night?" I asked.

He nodded.

"I thought Harold was letting me have a chance to see that Soul survives as the individual. That the individual is the true state of Soul."

Rebazar Tarzs turned to see the curious face of a black-and-white cat peering through an opening in the fence. The cat seemed caught between some inner desire to approach this ECK Master and its natural instincts for survival through safety. Rebazar Tarzs took a few steps and knelt down to scratch its furry ears, and the cat purred.

As I felt the power of the ECK Master's presence move with his attention to the cat, I began to wonder if indeed I had missed something very important from my experience.

Finally, he turned to me and said, "Now look, this Living ECK Master we have is a very subtle Master, and not many understand him. But I am going to be a bit more blunt when I say that he was trying to move you to that state where you could see the whole of Eckankar. You are close to catching it, and when you do, nothing will be able to shake it from you.

"One might think that after all these years of study you would have caught the secret, but remember, not many will reach that point in this lifetime. Look at all the masses of people on this planet. Look at movement after movement that continues to abuse and take advantage of the individual because they have not understood the secret.

"The one thing you should always remember is that all these movements, all these groups, are battling for the individual. They have found the secret that only Soul, the individual, is the central operating unit in the worlds of God. Nothing can happen except through Soul. Nothing can exist without It. The ECK, or reality, will only respond to Soul and nothing else. This means that whoever can capture Soul, as you might net the fish of the sea—as the Christians put it—will have the greatest power known.

"So why does man continually throw himself into groups and movements? He sees himself as a Christian, a Democrat, a Communist, or a thousand other designations, but never as Soul, the individual. He feels the need to belong, so he searches out a group consciousness. He dearly loves to live by rules and regulations, so he joins an organization. Alone, he feels helpless, so he takes part in some action team with high aspirations to change the world. This is Soul's way of looking for survival.

"But one day Soul outgrows these outer movements, which lose their fascination for It. Soul begins to ask questions such as: Who am I? Where am I going? But no one can answer them except the individual. Then Soul begins the long, hard road to extricate Itself from the group consciousness and regain Its individuality. This is when the ECK Masters step in to offer their assistance, and thus the path of ECK appears when the time is ripe. Now do you see how this all ties together?"

"I think so," I answered. "But then, how can there be an organization carrying the name of Eckankar? Isn't this a contradiction?"

"There is not much in this world that isn't," he said. "When the ECK, the Life Force, flows into this world It

265

takes every form. It might be a flower, a river, or a solar system. It might even be a mirage in the desert or a vision of God. The ECK flows into this world but never finds completion or perfection, so It is always changing: always dying in Its old forms to be born into the new. It might come together to produce a spiritual era, or It might hide for ages behind the traditional teachings. The ECK is all of life, so don't try to fit It into some little box.

"The Living ECK Master might use an organization if his mission dictates it, or he might work with a few close ones as a team. He is free to use whatever means he can. But the minute his followers begin to feel they are above others, the minute they begin to talk in "shoulds" or "should nots"—or limit in any way a person's individual path of truth—then they can become more of a hindrance than a help. He might try to lift them beyond these areas, but he cannot force them; and if the situation grows bad enough, he might just leave everything behind and walk the lonely hills by himself, searching for those who truly seek the Light of God.

"Now don't shake your head, because this has happened in the past and will happen again. This is indeed what makes for a contradiction. Thus, unless the seeker looks beneath the surface of what he sees, he may never glimpse the true teachings of ECK. He might miss what the Master is trying to tell him.

"OK. Now I want to go back to this subject of the ways that Soul searches for survival. If It cannot find survival through individuality, then Soul might find it in fame or infamy. In other words, if Soul can preserve Its image or name in the memories of others, then It might feel It has survival. Or It may find survival vicariously through fleshly offspring, such as the father or mother whose whole interest is the lives of their children.

"Soul might take up some job that It feels is important in the running of an organization. This can be Its mission, you see? Or It might choose survival in the feeling that It is one of the few who knows some secret, ages old. This is how the mystery schools have preserved themselves. They claim to be a brotherhood that has endured from the ancient days of civilization by passing down certain secrets. These secrets may not bring immortality, but the individual finds survival by feeling a part of this brotherhood.

"The point is that when Soul has a purpose or a goal, then It has survival. But when Soul accepts the dreams of others, It loses something vital. Once the individual begins to act out someone else's goal, or some purpose established for It by others, then the interest and affection It has for what It is doing becomes weakened. Do too much of this and Soul can lose the very source of inspiration and ideas that will lead It out of Its troubles and into the higher spiritual worlds.

"So you see, the true freedom of Soul to act upon Its wishes is the very origin of your power to succeed. The greater your goal, the greater your power to reach it. And out of this freedom and power comes the deepest love for every act you perform. These are the three aspects, as I have said before: freedom, power, and love.

"Now those who have said that harmony should come first and freedom second are wrong. Without freedom, harmony is an act or a show; but with freedom, harmony is the greatest expression of the divine law. This is what the movements of today have overlooked. They have hidden the secret that Soul is the central operating unit of life. This is why the individual is such a trampled-on unit in our modern world.

"So, if you wish to have freedom within the worlds of God, to become the spiritual traveler yourself, then you must first learn to control your own will. An undisciplined will is your worst enemy. Next, you must control your imagination; let nothing limit it, nor conform it. Last, you must begin to make contact with the spiritual power Itself. You must learn to live in the ECK and through It. The ECK Masters are always near those who are bold and adventuresome.

"This is some of what you should have gotten from the experience the Living ECK Master gave you!"

"I had no idea," I said.

The Tibetan nodded his head and pointed his finger at me. "There is always more to ECK than meets the eye," he said, and let out a hearty laugh that was infectious; it was so full of life.

10

Finding Your Spiritual Guide

Our spiritual guide appears when we are ready.

Search for God

K. Virginia Slagle

As a child, I was raised in the Baptist faith. But as I grew older, a divine discontent stirred within me; and my personal search for God began.

It led me through a variety of teachings: philosophy, world religions, mythology, parapsychology, hypnotism, Silva Mind Control, and the Rosicrucians. But a golden thread ran through all my experiences that eventually brought me to the teachings of ECK.

In 1970, I attended classes to develop my psychic abilities. We learned a visualization technique which felt like daydreaming. I was instructed to gaze upon the inner screen of my imagination and trust whatever appeared.

In one guided visualization exercise, we imagined an inner workroom and laboratory for ourselves. Mine stood on a cliff overlooking the ocean. In my imagination, I went outside. As I gazed over the panoramic view of my lab and the ocean beyond, a face appeared in the sky. It hung above the horizon, then flew toward me. Soon a full-sized man was standing on the path before me.

The visual clarity of this full-color image was astounding. The man had a tall white turban, dark piercing eyes, dark skin, and a close-cropped beard. He disappeared as quickly as he had arrived.

Another exercise brought me more surprises. Using the same technique, I imagined a large elevator door inside my laboratory. Our instructor told us that our personal guides, both male and female, would soon step through the elevator door.

The door slowly opened. I saw a short woman with light brown hair step from the elevator, greet me, and then busy herself about the room. I stood dumbfounded, wondering what to expect next.

I was told to use the same technique for the male guide, but this time the elevator door was painfully slow to open. Finally a slender man with dark brown hair appeared, neatly dressed in a light blue suit. He just stood in the center of the room, hands clasped behind his back, observing. I stammered trivialities to welcome him.

These experiences all seemed as real to me as my waking life, but our graduation exercise allowed me to test the truth of what I had seen. I was given the name and location of a physical subject and asked to describe the person and any health problems this person had.

At first, it felt as though I were making up the picture as I went along—just imagining it. But after a while, I clearly saw the outline of a man of medium build with blazing auburn hair. Nothing appeared wrong with his body except for a horizontal line above his left knee. His leg and foot below this point were outlined with a dotted line.

The classmate who had brought the information card on his friend verified the auburn hair, the build, and that the man's left leg had been amputated just above the knee. This was an important yardstick for me to measure my perceptions of inner realities.

By now I was frantic to find a path which suited me. I tried the Unitarian church, the Baha'i faith, the Church of God, and Fundamentalism. But nothing really fit.

In 1976, in between paths, I found the book, *ECKANKAR—The Key to Secret Worlds,* by the modern-day founder of Eckankar, Paul Twitchell. The ECK teachings fascinated me, but at the time, I could find no other books or news of the organization. So I began studying with the Rosicrucians.

A year later, in a local bookstore, I found *The Tiger's Fang,* also by Paul Twitchell. In the back was information on how to get more books about Eckankar. Between study lessons from the Rosicrucians, I was glued to my new ECK study materials, which I had received through the mail.

When the Rosicrucians asked me to take a loyalty oath to continue my studies with them, I just couldn't do it. I was dropped from their membership rolls; shortly thereafter, I met one of the three members of Eckankar who lived in my small northern California town. I was startled to recognize her as the petite lady with light brown hair whom I had seen on the inner elevator earlier! She and her husband answered hundreds of my questions about Eckankar. I also learned that Paul Twitchell, author of so many of my favorite ECK books, had died in 1971.

Not long after this, I recognized the turbaned man, who had appeared to me by the inner seashore, in a painting of ECK Masters featured in an Eckankar publication. Perhaps I studied the ECK teachings with him in another life.

The face of the third person, the man in the light blue suit, was unknown to me until 1981, when the spiritual leadership of ECK was passed to Sri Harold Klemp, the 973rd (and present) Mahanta, the Living ECK Master. I recognized him as the man who appeared through the elevator doors; he was my inner guide so many years before.

In the ECK teachings it is said that one's faith in the Inner Master and in one's own knowingness is the key to experiencing inner realities. I am grateful for all the outer confirmation I have received about my deepest inner experiences.

The Word

Cybil Fisher

At fifteen, I have often wondered how I could serve God in my daily life. Recently I was given the opportunity without even knowing it. It wasn't until afterward that I realized, Hey, I served the ECK!

I have a friend who is not a member of Eckankar. One day we were talking about the recent death of a close friend. As I shared my thoughts on death, I could see she was puzzled. The views I expressed were very different from Christian ideas, so I explained a little about Eckankar to her. She was interested and asked a lot of questions.

My friend went home and told her mother about Eckankar. A strict Christian, her mother told her Christianity was the only true path to God. Still my friend wondered, Is Eckankar for me? She came to me with her question. All I could say was, "I guess that's a question you must answer for yourself."

A couple of days later, she called me. She'd had an experience that helped her decide about ECK. She was lying in bed thinking of the differences between Eckankar and Christianity. "Which is better for me?"

275

she wondered aloud. She closed her eyes to think about it.

Suddenly she felt a change in the atmosphere. She opened her eyes and saw a large Blue Light at the foot of her bed. Within the Blue Light stood a man. She had never seen the man before, yet it seemed that she knew him. As soon as she blinked her eyes, he and the light were gone. Then softly, musically, almost inaudibly, a word came to her.

Later, she came to me to ask what the word meant. When I told her, she knew that Eckankar was right for her. The word? It was *Wah Z,* the spiritual name of the Living ECK Master, Harold Klemp.

Fork in the Road

Margaret Slattery

Before I found Eckankar, I studied with a teacher in Hawaii who possessed extraordinary psychic powers. As one of his first students and ministers, I settled into the role of psychic counselor for his metaphysical church. Adept at reading auras and psychic scanning, I counseled friends and strangers by probing their most private depths. Healings were commonplace. I would simply drop the name of the afflicted person into our "healing circle" for miraculous cures.

Now, this is true sainthood, I pridefully mused, as I noted my "spiritual" accomplishments and awed friends.

But the psychic powers we unleashed were starting to cast dark shadows. Several students committed suicide. My teacher began to manipulate his followers for money, sex, and psychic influence. My health started to suffer from the many "healings" I'd performed. Actually, I had simply interfered with the sick individuals' karma and taken it upon myself.

I didn't know my teacher had failed a test of power. He was spiraling down into darkness and taking all of

277

us with him. I was a psychic prisoner and didn't know it!

During this turbulent time, I cried out to Spirit for help. An interesting dream followed. I found myself next in line to see a Master. Her aura of love left my knees shaking, and I dropped to the rug before her. She sat on a beautifully brocaded pillow, radiating a soft corona of light that danced about her head. Her voice sounded like velvety water; it poured over me like a waterfall. "You are unfolding like a flower," she said with gentleness. Her wisdom flowed from the depths of Soul.

A highly polished table caught her reflection as she leaned over to deftly pluck a single blue carnation from its vase. In one fluid motion, she deposited the flower in my hand. I was embarrassed at taking the only flower on her table. She smiled understandingly.

"Choose," the Master whispered softly, as her slender fingers pointed to many trinkets neatly arranged around the vase. I gingerly reached for a tiny crystal figure of a blue man. I awoke with the feeling that it was still clutched reverently in my palm.

I looked forward to our next dream meeting, but it never came. This mysterious being had pointed out my next spiritual step. Six months would pass before I realized the significance of this inner experience.

The dream led to my resignation from the metaphysical church. My teacher was outraged and refused to let me go. In his anger, he began a battery of psychic assaults that left me weak and fearing for my sanity.

When my second pregnancy failed, my world caved in. I no longer had the strength or the will to fight my teacher. One day his attacks broke through from the inner planes to the physical world. One moment I was gazing at the waves on the outer reefs far below my apartment window. The next moment I was hurled into a realm of collapsed time. Mountains of electrical energy erupted around me, sending needles of pain through my back.

I spun around and met a thunderous blow across the face! Wave after wave of blows sent me ricocheting against the walls of this unearthly realm. It was like being shredded alive. Desperately I fought to stay conscious and survive. The glimpses of the monster attacking me left me terrified. Its center fumed in an electrical darkness of unspeakable depths, exploding around in a raging storm of red-and-black lightning. I recoiled in horror as I glimpsed the face of my old teacher!

The aftershocks of the attack reverberated to my core. Something inside of me snapped alive, fighting to reach consciousness. I remembered *something*. What was it? I frantically clawed at the memory, but my mind was numb.

As I sank deeper into the pit of terror, I screamed out for help. "Oh, God! Please hear me!" A true Master would hear me, wouldn't he? The ground broke under me, and a swirling funnel of no thought, sight, or feeling began to pull me toward its abysmal depths.

Almost in the same instant, someone grabbed me from behind and tossed me a hundred feet upward, as easily as a child would toss a doll. My rescuer was a brightly illuminated being made up of blue sparkles. He wasted no time in engaging in combat with the angry mass of red-and-black lightning before him. He looked so small against the huge hulk of my former teacher.

Yet I could feel his power even from the distance that separated us. In the split second that I perceived his beauty and power, I found myself back in my body at home—a shaking, nauseous mass of quivering nerves. But I knew that "my" Master was real now. His love followed me for many days, erasing all fear of my old teacher. I had finally seen the power of true love. All of my magic tricks had proved useless until this love broke the chains of fear that had held me prisoner.

Not long after that, I found the Outer Master, the Living ECK Master. I recognized his photograph on the back cover of a book and ventured into the local Eckankar Center to find out more. A woman there told me the picture was of Sri Harold Klemp, the present spiritual leader of Eckankar. I could never forget the face of my rescuer. I had finally found my teacher.

Life wasn't all roses after that initial recognition of the Inner and Outer Master. Many changes shook my life as years of meditation gave way to the Spiritual Exercises of ECK.

Now my days are spent as an active participant in life. The sleeping hours are an opportunity to consciously explore my inner worlds. Soul Travel is so different and so far superior to psychic phenomena that it must be experienced to be believed!

I could never return to playing with power and psychic tricks. There is so much beyond the psychic realms; I don't want to be bound there anymore. And though old friends don't understand my new path, forging on alone has brought me many new bonds. The pure Light of ECK far outshines any of the phenomenal experiences I had while on the dark fork in the road. If I listen to my inner guidance, I know I will avoid any obstacles on the path; if I fall flat on my face, Wah Z (Sri Harold Klemp's spiritual name) is always there to pick me up, a knowing smile on his face.

Sri Harold Klemp has passed the tests we now face and is the Mahanta, the Living ECK Master—

symbolized for me in the inner worlds by the single blue carnation. It's good to know we have competent help from the ECK Masters on the long, twisting, and sometimes surprising road home to God.

Journey Out of Darkness

Susan Hanniford Crowley

In that awkward place where I wasn't really a child but not quite an adult, I experienced a very real pain, an inner anguish. Anguish and adolescence seem to go together. I wanted so much to be liked by others for myself but had no idea who I was inside. During this confusing time I searched for my answers in witchcraft and magic.

I didn't know at the time how dangerous and damaging the occult can be. It can destroy your health, your sense of well-being, and corrupt your values and ideals. You can lose everything through it.

My justification was to label what I was doing as white magic. I was deluding myself—there is no such thing as white magic. Whenever we intend to have power over others, no matter for what reason, we are practicing black magic. When we attempt to use magic for beneficial results, we create a debt to Spirit. Even praying for a terminally ill person can do harm. Prayers can hold that Soul in a dying body against Its will, interfering with Its freedom of choice.

After I finally left the occult sciences, I spent three

years searching. Those years weighed on my heart like three centuries, as I suffered tragedy and disaster in karmic payment for my meddling. Black magic returned under a new guise: hypnotism. I learned of the deep deception involved in allowing another to control you and quit as soon as I realized it was another form of darkness. I studied many paths and religions, hoping to find a faint glimmer of God's Light.

I found that light in an ECKist's eyes. I had to know what made him sparkle so! The happiness and strong reliance on an inner source of love and wisdom reflected in his view of life and the way he treated others. He told me how I could experience God's love, the ECK, through the daily Spiritual Exercises of Eckankar. People talked a lot about believing, but I was ready to experience Spirit firsthand.

When I chose to start my journey in the Light and Sound, I was given the gift of an Inner Guide, the Mahanta. This friend loves me without judging me by my mistakes. And from him I can learn the answers of life directly from its source.

The Mahanta and I spent years working together to repair the injuries I suffered through my occult experiences—I witnessed the process in occasional nightmares. Gradually the pain and fear were replaced with understanding, joy, and self-confidence. All this was to prepare me for a moment of truth I would soon have to face, in order to pay my debts to Spirit.

My dream life took a strange turn. First a claw reached out of the darkness for me. Then I had night terrors, awakening each morning in a cold sweat. Night after night my nightmares intensified, culminating in one terrifying dream.

In the dream, chains gripped my arms, legs, and waist; each held by a group of people dressed in black.

As I tried to struggle forward, they pulled on the bonds, crying: "You must stay with us. You belong to us." I screamed and pulled with all my strength but couldn't break free. I was in the lobby of a luxury hotel, but no one appeared to notice what was happening to me.

Through a doorway I saw the Mahanta, the Living ECK Master in a small lobby talking with a group of people. The entrance of the lobby was guarded by two men, who stopped me as I struggled to enter. One of them said, "I'm sorry, Miss, but you can't pass through." I tried to push my way into the room but the people in black pulled all the harder at the chains wrapped around my limbs. To make things worse, the Master was apparently getting ready to leave. Hope was dying in me. Tears streamed down my face, and I cried out, "Mahanta, help me!"

Immediately he turned and came toward me. As he offered his hand and I accepted it—the chains evaporated! I walked through the door to the guarded lobby and continued on with the Mahanta, never looking back.

The terrors in the night ended with that dream. My deep wounds from the occult had finally healed. If we are willing to reach for the Light and Sound, symbolized for me by the hand of the Mahanta, the ECK can dissolve whatever is holding us back and light the deepest cavern of the heart. The Mahanta is there for every Soul who chooses to make the journey out of darkness.

Startling Meeting

Marsha Gibson

I met Sri Harold Klemp in 1981. I was in Los Angeles for my husband's Army reunion. My first novel was scheduled to be published, and, on a whim, I phoned a book promoter I had met at a seminar. He agreed to meet with me, so my husband and I took a taxi to his hotel where a convention was being held.

In the lobby, authors were gathered around the book promoter. As they chatted, I glimpsed a man with dark brown hair and glasses talking to the promoter. Even from behind I recognized the man—that is, I knew him but couldn't place where we'd met.

When I saw his face, I was certain I knew him and almost touched my husband on the arm to say, "There's that man I am always saying so-and-so looks like." I caught myself just in time, realizing how strange that would sound. I stood there trying to figure out just who he could be—so familiar that I occasionally described other men as resembling him.

Over the noise of the group of people, I heard the book promoter, whose face was lit with special pleasure, ask the man with glasses if he wished to be introduced as *Sri* Harold Klemp. I had never heard the word *Sri* before. His soft voice answered, "Just Harold Klemp." Each of the authors was introduced, but no one seemed to notice *him*.

Conversation bubbled again, and I couldn't help staring at him. Then I turned and found him standing beside me. His eyes were very special and powerful. I couldn't shake the strong feeling of familiarity and affection that enveloped me. To begin a conversation I said, "I'm sorry, I can't remember your name."

"Harold Klemp."

My head was in a turmoil; a lot going on in there somewhere. I also had trouble speaking, which was strange.

"That's a hard name," I said lamely, wondering why my brain felt so rusty. "Would you say it again?" He did. "Would you spell it for me?" And he did.

"What is the title of your book?" I asked next.

"The Wind of Change."

"What is it about?" I felt I was asking dumb questions, but I had to keep a conversation going.

He looked full at me now, and a most extraordinary thing happened. The full force of his gaze sent a powerful electric charge coursing through me. The waves were visible, rippling down a tunnel toward and past me, like corrugations. There was a quiet roar and a feeling of coolness in the touch of that mysterious energy. The world outside my tunnel had disappeared. "Have you ever heard of Eckankar?" he asked.

I struggled to answer because the machinery of my brain had turned to dust—it was barely functioning. However, I was not afraid. It was as if I had expected all my life that something like this might happen (although not that weekend!)

I relaxed and felt the cool waves of force wash through me. Somehow I knew what I said next would be important.

"What is it?" I asked, knowing I was asking a lot more than a simple question.

"An international spiritual organization," he responded.

"Would you spell it?" I hoped he did not mind my requests to spell everything. It was hard for me to register the words because of the waves of energy sweeping toward me, engulfing me. I wondered how on earth I was going to explain this to my husband and looked for him, but my spouse was trapped in a conversation.

I don't remember exactly how he moved away, but I kept watching him as the others chatted around me. He stood on the fringes of the group, arms folded, preoccupied as if daydreaming. Oddly, no one else seemed to notice him. After a while, I looked again, and he was gone.

I couldn't share my experience with my beloved husband because there was no logical way to describe it. But for the remaining three days in Los Angeles, I walked in happiness, skimming the floors and sidewalks with little contact. I gave an impromptu speech that weekend and was surprised to hear myself speaking of love and of touching those special feelings deep inside us.

It was six months before I found the book, *In My Soul I Am Free* on a library shelf, and a year and a half before I felt the urge to go searching for more information on Eckankar. When I finally found the courage to walk in the door of the Eckankar Center, no one could have been more surprised than I. There in the corner, a picture was sitting atop the small table. It was my "mysterious Master," for I had so dubbed him in my thoughts. I knew I had found the path home.

The Secret Dream Message

Jeff Timpe

In the dream, I seated myself in what seemed to be more of an auditorium than a church, with seats and a stage. A prophet had already begun to speak on stage before we came in. I remember thinking that his face resembled that of Moses. The audience's attention was then drawn to a man center-stage giving a demonstration of "astral acrobatics." His arms were tied to stabilize his body, and he was levitating off the ground.

After absorbing a few pointers, I found myself attempting to levitate out of my chair, without the support of training wires. After much concentration and effort, I managed to levitate above my seat, about level with the heads of the people in the audience. Happy with my progress, I shouted, "Look at me!"

The master on stage pointed his finger and proclaimed, "A resemblance of a mustard seed!" The audience chuckled, and I, relating to the comment, sank back into my chair with a feeling of happiness and humor at my display of "faith."

At that point I realized that my efforts created the struggle, and correcting my attitude, I easily and happily soared above the audience. I soon approached the speaker and stopped to embrace him, as a gesture of thanks.

The embrace was transformed into an emotional bond between student and Master. I immediately visualized our hearts expanding with dazzling white light and connecting into a solid shaft of white.

Without words, the embrace communicated the essence of all my feelings, triumphs, frustrations—the whole drama of my life on earth—in one emotional burst. "Yes, I know, my son," was his soft and comforting reply, and I sighed in relief and devotion.

I was then given a torn portion of a program on which he wrote the name HAROD KLEMP. When saying it, he pronounced the name with the *L* in Harold, yet omitted it in writing. He wrote the name twice so I would not forget.

Upon awakening, I had a pretty good memory of this experience from the other side. The name Harold Klemp was uppermost in my thoughts, clear as a bell. It sounded so familiar, yet I couldn't place it; but I soon discovered from a ticket to an Eckankar seminar that it was the name of the Living ECK Master. What an affirmation to a semiskeptical seeker like myself!

Needless to say, my attendance at the seminar was not in question!

Feeling the Presence
of the Master

Debra Midyette

With the eagerness of a child awaiting a gift, I had counted the days until the 1986 ECKANKAR Creative Arts Festival in New Orleans. My trip, funded by a timely tax return, would provide my first opportunity to see and hear the Living ECK Master.

As the first day of the seminar slipped past, each speaker and creative arts presentation heightened my awareness of Spirit. I felt so much love, like being at a family reunion.

Finally came the moment I had awaited so eagerly. Sri Harold Klemp, the Living ECK Master, stepped to a chair midstage and began his talk of spiritual parables, humor, and insights. I felt like a sponge as I tried to absorb his every word.

But I wondered what, if any, effect this seminar would have on me. Several longtime students of Eckankar had told me of their first meeting with the Master. Some had felt the glow of his radiant love. Others had lapsed into a light sleep or experienced the

Light and Sound of God during his talk. But nothing of the sort was happening to me. What was wrong? Hadn't I practiced the Spiritual Exercises of ECK correctly?

Just as my worries started to get the best of me, I heard the familiar voice of the Inner Master: "Let go, Debra. Just listen." So I relaxed and enjoyed the rest of the talk, taking comfort in the fact that there were two more occasions to hear Sri Harold speak before the end of the seminar.

After the main program, I attended a workshop on the spiritual meaning of dreams. At the door I ran into a new acquaintance who casually teased me about my pale skin. (I live at the beach but don't sport a suntan.) We joked awhile and then went into the workshop.

The dream class began, and I listened intently to each of the speakers. About midway through the first hour, my face began to feel warm, as if I were blushing. Distracted by tingling sensations in my arms and legs, I looked down and saw that my skin was turning bright pink. During a short break in the workshop my friend spotted me and exclaimed, "Wow! I take back that comment about pale skin. You look like you have a whopping sunburn!" By then it felt like one, too: my arms and legs were glowing with color.

As I walked to my room that evening, I mulled over the many insights the day had yielded and felt fortunate to have attended this spiritual seminar. My skin still burned, but I decided it was an allergic reaction to some spicy Cajun food from earlier that day.

But I was wrong. As I undressed for bed, I stared at my reddened skin in the mirror with real bewilderment. Only the exposed portions of my body were red. It looked as if I had sunbathed for hours wearing my blouse and skirt. How could this be?

The inner radiance of the Master had left me with a tan from the Light of God. My first encounter with the Living ECK Master turned out to be a unique experience after all.

Thank God He Came Along!

Katherine Helmerssen

Mum said she could never believe in anything she couldn't see, without proof. Patiently, without pushing, a series of events revealed to us how the ECK works miracles in our daily lives.

She had tried to read a few books on Eckankar without success. But one day, she again asked for an ECK book, so I gave her *Hello Friend* by Patti Simpson. Mum read the whole book in one day.

Afterward, she came to me smiling happily and made a casual remark about how the ECK was helping me to be more creative. I remember being pleased that she felt comfortable with my involvement in Eckankar. Little did I know the way was being prepared for one of life's greatest adventures.

A few months later she mentioned a bad dream of the previous night. I asked her to tell me about it.

"I dreamed about a tiger. He came charging into the house. Dad grabbed a rifle, but it wouldn't go off. He was grappling with the tiger on the floor. A policeman came but couldn't shoot the tiger for fear of hurting Dad. I woke up feeling very stiff and tense."

Almost as an afterthought, she added, "In the end, a clergyman came along and said, 'Don't worry, I killed the tiger.' "

"What did the clergyman look like?" I inquired eagerly.

Mum stared at me, her mouth falling open. Slowly she said, "You don't think it was..."

"The Living ECK Master once studied to be a clergyman. Did he wear glasses?" (Sri Harold Klemp then wore dark-rimmed glasses.)

"Yes," she answered slowly.

I showed her a photo of Sri Harold Klemp, who had just become the Living ECK Master.

"Did he look like this?" I asked.

"Yes, he did—that's him!"

As she rose to leave, my mother added to herself, "Thank God he came along."

I recorded this incident in my diary of dreams and spiritual contemplations, grateful the ECK was protecting her.

About three weeks later, I received an urgent call from the hospital. Mum had suffered a massive coronary. As I entered the room where she lay heavily sedated, I saw a blue light shining softly against her left eye. The Master was at hand.

For two days she clung to the physical, while her loved ones drew near. Only once, when I was alone with her, was she at all conscious. Speaking slowly and clearly, I asked if she recalled the man who had saved Dad from the tiger. She answered by twitching her mouth slightly. His spiritual name is Wah Z, I told her, and if she needed his help, all she need do was call him. She twitched her mouth again; I knew she understood.

The medical staff arrived to check her, so I stepped out of the room for a moment. When I returned, Mum was in a deep sleep. There was a marked change in her appearance. Her whole being literally shone with a deep peace and beauty, and I knew she was gaining the help she needed to cross over to the other side. She was in loving hands.

My Initiation into ECKANKAR

Darcy Hoover

I was first introduced to Eckankar by a very dear
friend who had been raised an ECKist. She told
me about the Light and the Sound and explained some
of the principles of ECK to me.

Shortly after that, I received my first introduction
to the Inner Master, the Mahanta, in my dreams. It
came at a time when I was quite ill and was spending a
lot of time sleeping. I had a dream in which I was in a
crowded room, watching a sea of faces move past me.
As I watched the blur I caught glimpses of a slim,
dark-haired man standing among the crowd. He was
looking right at me and smiling a wonderful smile that
filled me with a love I will never forget. Then he was
gone. As I look back now, this dream seems to have
been a sneak preview of a more formal introduction
which was to follow.

Some months later, I had another dream in which my
friend and I were standing in a corridor outside a
lecture hall. We were discussing where we would go for
lunch when a gentleman approached us. "Good afternoon," he said in a quiet voice. "I am Harold Klemp, the

301

Mahanta, the Living ECK Master." He extended his hand and greeted us warmly.

We began to introduce ourselves, but he was already calling us by name and saying, "I have heard of you two." His eyes were full of light, and his presence filled me with warmth. He said that he hoped we would enjoy his lecture, then he bade us farewell and vanished as quickly as he had appeared. In the dream, my friend and I then went to lunch and exchanged reactions, vowing never to wash our hands again because he had touched them.

When I told my friend about this dream, she was happy for me. She said that when a person is ready, the Master will appear to them. I then realized the importance of this dream, and quite honestly, I felt honored.

In the days that followed I began to notice the ECK in my everyday life. I could see the Light and hear the divine Sound in my inner ear. I began to feel a circle of warmth around me whenever I thought about the ECK. Six months later, after seeing the ECK consistently prove Itself in my life, I became a member of Eckankar. I am nineteen now and have not had a dream with the Master since, but I know he is always with me.

Sent Back to Life

Gabriel Abiye Pikibo

I was traveling on business from Port Harcourt to Lagos, Nigeria, when I woke one morning with a severe illness. I had the hotel call an ambulance, which rushed me to the nearest hospital. I was explaining my condition to the doctor when suddenly everything went black.

I awoke in a dream. I was in a very long, fast-moving line. All the people were passing through a checkpoint. But when my turn to pass came, I was pulled aside and sent back by a slim white man.

When I woke up, I was told I had just spent the previous ten days in a coma. The hospital had refused my body and sent me to another clinic, believing that all hope was lost. The clinic in which I found myself was a teaching clinic, and the doctors were only studying my body. They had cut the toe of my right leg—the only place where a single vein was still alive—and set up an intravenous drip. They did not expect me to revive.

I stayed in the clinic an additional three days before I was discharged. The doctors said my recovery was truly amazing—an act of God. Friends and relatives in

Lagos began to call me by a different form of my name to signify my rebirth into life.

When I finally traveled back to Port Harcourt, my wife could not believe I was alive. She'd had an experience the night I blacked out. She had awakened to the sound of someone knocking on the door. But when she opened it no one was there. It must have been a dream, she said to herself. She walked outside to calm herself and heard my voice calling her. Seeing no one, she ran back inside the house full of fear.

Later that night I appeared to her in the dream state. I told her certain people were behind my death and warned her to look at the behavior of these people during the funeral arrangements. She even remembered seeing the coffin that contained my body.

Actually, I knew I had gone into the beyond during this experience. I never forgot the face of the white man who sent me back to life, but I refused to tell anybody about the experience.

In Africa, we believe that ancestors can sometimes send children, who meet untimely deaths, back to life. Folklore has it that the child then owes some kind of debt to the Soul on the other side.

I thought this was what happened to me, but I did not believe I had ever been related to a white man. How did this come about? The question repeated itself to me many times, but no answer came. I never asked anybody because I knew they couldn't give me a satisfactory answer.

Then in February of 1985, I attended my first Eckankar gathering at Port Harcourt. I read brochures and attended several ECK activities. Later that day, I decided to follow the path of Eckankar. It did not occur to me that my experience with death was linked to Eckankar until recently. Yet it came as a fire into my heart when I read the *ECKANKAR Journal*. There I saw a picture of the Mahanta, Sri Harold Klemp. The slim man that saved my life was the Living ECK Master!

The Master was with me and protected me even before I knew about Eckankar. I know the love and protection of the Mahanta is very real.

11

Experiences in the Light and Sound

New worlds open up to us with the Master's help.

A Soul Travel Visit to the Other Worlds

Robert Scott Rochek

I had a Soul Travel experience at the 1986 Eckankar International Creative Arts Festival in New Orleans. Now I know that the Mahanta's presence is always with me. But it's still up to me to let go of the small, physical state of consciousness and allow the God-self to unfold within me.

I was attending a workshop on how to visit the Temples of Golden Wisdom on the inner spiritual planes. As we were led through a visualization technique, I consciously met Wah Z* and Tibetan ECK Master Rebazar Tarzs near the Temple of Golden Wisdom in the city of Retz on Venus.

The Soul Travel experience began with a faint scent of sandalwood. Suddenly I was standing on a white-marble path surrounded by beautiful flowers. As I glanced to the left, I saw a golden light laced with

---

*The spiritual name of Sri Harold Klemp, the Living ECK Master.

glowing violet. Wah Z was there, and he introduced me to Rebazar Tarzs. The Tibetan ECK Master looked penetratingly into my eyes and said, "Now your true journey into the worlds of God shall begin. Will you submit to my guidance and do as I say?"

"Yes, Sri Tarzs, I will!"

"Will you abide by the word of the Mahanta?" he asked.

I turned to Wah Z and said, "Yes, Mahanta, I will!"

Then Wah Z told me to step into the swirling light. As I did this, the brilliant gold-and-violet light spiraled up and around and through me, penetrating every cell.

"Now you are filled with the Light and Sound of ECK," declared Rebazar. "All will be well with you!" He led me up the steps of marble into the Temple of Golden Wisdom.

Wah Z was by my side as I entered a small room to the right of the main chamber. It was brilliantly lit from within by golden-white light. As I moved toward the light, I saw a rectangular marble pedestal about two feet wide and three feet high. Atop it rested a transparent glasslike container, filled with glowing script in an unknown tongue. It seemed as if one could read from this form of the Shariyat-Ki-Sugmad via energy imprints of Light and Sound.

On closer inspection, the writing seemed to be moving—alive and changing within the box, which was filled with a fluid, viscous substance. Telepathically, Wah Z told me that this Shariyat wasn't read like words on a page. Rather, one simply touched the box with one's hands, and waves of Spirit-filled Sound and Light were transmitted directly into the chela. This was a most astounding realization to me!

Meanwhile in the physical body, I was sitting in the

310

workshop writing furiously, with one eye on the inner and the other on the page before me. As I placed my hands on the Shariyat-Ki-Sugmad, this is what was transmitted, as I experienced and recorded it:

"The Shariyat-Ki-Sugmad is the condensed Sound and Light of ECK in a form that is tangible and can be understood by beings while in the inner planes. It is the actual wisdom of SUGMAD (God), that part of the vibrations of ECK which that particular section of the Shariyat represents. This is why one can touch one of these forms of the Shariyat and have the vibration, or wisdom, of that particular Shariyat transmitted directly into him—Sound and Light being what the Shariyat really is."

But the most important part of this Soul Travel experience came after I returned again to the workshop. The speaker asked if any were willing to share their inner journeys. At first I was hesitant, but the Mahanta let me know that it would be for the greatest good to tell others, and I did. As I stood to speak, the students nearest me passed a microphone, so all could hear. I realized that they had accompanied me to the pedestal of the Shariyat. Now they were eager to hear of my experience and confirm their own inner journeys.

As I read the message given me, many faces lit up. I felt we were joined together on this path of the Golden Heart.

After the workshop a young man came up to me with his eyes agleam. He had often visited this same wisdom temple but had been frustrated in his attempts to read the living Shariyat as if it were an ordinary book. Because I had been allowed to help others learn, I experienced such gratitude and love from this Soul. He had finally learned the secret of placing his hands on the surface of the Shariyat, so now the ECK within it could flow to him via the Golden Heart. He gained something he'd wanted for a long time, and by being a channel for ECK, I gained more than words can ever express.

I was shown how the greater experiences of spiritual worth come from giving—not from the little self, which continually demands to receive. I look forward to each moment in the nowness of eternity with the Mahanta, as I unfold in conscious awareness of Divine Spirit and the God-self within me.

From Psychic Healer
to ECK Traveler

Marion White

Some of us are born into this life with a sensitivity to the invisible levels. When I was young, I began my adventures in the inner, invisible worlds, yet it was many years before I was ready for the teachings of Eckankar.

As a small child I was frightened of the dark. Colors came zooming out of the darkness, making weird noises. But as I lay down to sleep each night, I became aware of a man sitting on a chair beside my bed. I knew I was safe because of his presence, and he did not frighten me, even though I could see right through him.

Over the years he became my companion in the sleep state, and we traveled together to marvelous places. I visited blue-skinned people and saw a tunnel that looked like a temple of Egyptian design. During these travels, I began to learn the lessons that would prepare me for meeting the Living ECK Master years later.

An early step in my spiritual development was an ability to see the future. One of my friends, Janice, played a game where she would jump from wall to wall in the gardens on our street. I could foresee her slipping and cutting her right knee. I warned her to stop, but she would never take any notice.

One day I saw the vision sharply and begged her, "Janice, please do not jump that wall today. Today is the day you are going to slip."

"Pooh," said Janice. She jumped, slipped, and cut her right knee.

That was the day I lost all my friends: they thought I was a witch. I was almost eleven years old at the time, and I quickly learned to keep my predictions to myself. I found that if you can see into the future, friends are very happy to hear the good things that may happen to them. But they do not like bad tidings.

Another step in my spiritual journey came in my teen years. My father bought me a budgie, a parakeet. I named him Timmy, and this bundle of sky-blue feathers soon made himself a pampered member of the family. But in his seventh year, he had a stroke which paralyzed one side of his body. He lived another day and night. Oh, how I prayed that he would recover.

Then realizing how selfish I was being, I prayed to God and asked if He would take Timmy to heaven. But before my feathered friend left, I wanted to say good-bye.

That night I went to sleep with the prayer on my lips. In the early hours of the morning I was gently awakened by a monk dressed in a dark brown robe. A golden light radiated around him, and his kindly face lit my bedroom with a soft glow.

He said, "Come. It is time; you must say farewell to your little friend."

I followed him downstairs and picked up Timmy to

say good-bye. He held on to me tightly with his good foot.

Then the monk said, "You must go back to your room. Time grows short, and Timmy must be prepared for his journey ahead."

So I put Timmy back in his cage and went back to my room. After a while I felt a cool breeze pass over me.

We buried Timmy's body in the garden later that day. I cried for a week. At the end of the week the monk came back and woke me again. "Timmy cannot rest with you upsetting yourself like this," he said. "It has been decided to let you visit him."

Before us appeared the most beautiful garden I have ever seen. It was filled with all sorts of animals and people of every color and race, all smiling and at peace. Timmy was flying about in the trees.

Timmy made me understand that all was well with him. I was not to be sad about his passing. Although his physical body was dead, in spirit he was very much alive.

Then the monk said to me, "You must return to your home." And so we turned and walked along a bright beam of white light. When we arrived back in my room, the monk faded away.

The following morning, I was at peace. An important understanding had come to me. I knew now that we do not fade away into nothingness when we make the long journey home.

Many years later, when I was thirty-three, I began looking in earnest for my path to God. I decided to become a healer. My inner voice told me I would have to learn how to generate love within myself, and I was given instructions.

As I worked on expressing love, I suddenly discovered I could see people's auras. While waiting for the bus one day, I watched people on the other side of the road. Some people's auras were gray and narrow, while others were bright and wide.

As my inner sight developed, I was able to see disease manifested in the auras of different people. One day the man who sat next to me at work got up to get himself a cup of tea. On his right sleeve, in line with his elbow, was a dark mauve stain. I said, "Ron, you have put your elbow on a rubber-stamp pad. It's stained dark mauve."

He looked and said, "No, I haven't."

"Yes, you have," said I, looking again.

He got his cup of tea and returned to his desk. When he passed by again, the stain had disappeared. I later learned what it had been: he mentioned he had had a very painful elbow. This sort of inner sight went on for several years. For a time I found it very useful in my work as a healer.

I soon joined a spiritual church. As a vehicle of healing, I visualized the love of God flowing through me to others, and many got well. But other healers in the church resented this. People got better too quickly, and they were left without any patients. They asked me to leave the church, which I did. I then joined a spiritual development group run by a well-known medium in southern England.

After three years, I discovered I had become the channel, or source of spiritual power, for this group. I could not switch it off, nor could I control it. It was ruling my life and exhausting me. This was the last hold of the psychic worlds on me. I was now ready for the next step.

A friend had given me a book called *The Tiger's Fang,* by Eckankar's modern-day founder, Paul Twitchell. Reading the descriptions of his inner journeys to the different levels of heaven was like coming home. Here were the world of blue-skinned people and the Egyptian-style tunnel that I had known as a child. Someone else had experienced the same adventures!

I wrote the current Living ECK Master, Sri Harold Klemp, for help with my problem involving the spiritual development group I had become involved with. Shortly after, Sri Harold freed me from this group on the inner, invisible planes. I was then able to retire from the outer group. I was now ready to become a member of Eckankar and did so in August of 1984.

Psychic healing no longer holds any appeal for me. Now if people ask me for healing, I keep a detached attitude. I tell them that if they are meant to be healed, God will heal them. It may come through a doctor or some other person, or it may come in ways they do not recognize. Sometimes I suggest they contact the Mahanta, the Living ECK Master for help. All it takes is an open mind and a sincere inner request to him for guidance.

I've found that one can serve as a vehicle for God by simply listening to another's troubles. It is not necessary to unwittingly take on their karma through laying on of hands or other psychic means. If Soul has been awakened via the daily Spiritual Exercises of ECK, listening in a detached way to another's problems often allows Divine Spirit to touch them as It will. People will sometimes tell me their woes while waiting at the bus stop or riding on the train. Afterward, they say how much better they feel!

Subtle spiritual experiences such as these happen in my daily life now as well as in my dreams. With the

Spiritual Exercises of Eckankar, I am learning how to consciously slip into higher states, to work in harmony with all life. ECK has already taken me much farther than my psychic experiences and studies ever could have.

A Ride through the Universe

Richard J. Roberts

In the fall of 1971, I was a junior in high school and a very interested, active member of a fundamentalist Christian church. However, I continually argued in Sunday school. Always striving for the truth, I often poked holes in the logic of my teachers.

One day, a missionary from Nicaragua visited our church. He spoke through an interpreter. Someone asked him about Spirit. He said, "Spirit? That's not important. What I need is money for my project."

When I heard that, an exploding awareness raced up my spine, through my neck, and literally knocked me blind. Spirit was much more important than money! I left my body and shot through the roof of the church, crying out, "If God exists, show me the Holy Spirit now! I cannot tolerate such untruths!"

An inner voice soothed me, saying, "Things will be all right." I didn't like the answer, but I did calm down.

Later that evening several students and I stood around the parking lot of the church discussing the speaker's talk. As the others chatted, I noticed a dark, swarthy man walking toward us from the service station across the street. Two thoughts flashed into my mind: This man walks like a king; and if he walks any nearer, where am I going to run? I mentally mapped out escape routes, but forced myself not to act on the impulse to flee.

The man boldly stepped up to our circle and asked, "What are you discussing?" I turned and said, "We're talking about matters of Spirit. Do you have any observations?"

He calmly answered, "Yes." I can't remember what he said, but I do recall there was no way to argue with him. He answered each question with unassailable logic. He punctuated his words with quick movements of his hands, and his dark eyes flashed with animation. Little did I know that this man was none other than the great Tibetan ECK Master, Rebazar Tarzs.

Dimly I heard the man say he had heard me arguing in class that day. "The way you argued and handled yourself was extremely good. I liked what you said," he said simply.

Then he invited me to come hear a speaker. He emphasized that the speaker wasn't a preacher. "He won't try to change your religion; he won't try to sway your thinking. He's not into hypnosis, and he's not into the occult. Come listen to him," he beckoned. Because this speaker would be discussing matters of Spirit, I decided to go.

I followed the man with the flashing eyes across the street and down into the basement of another church. The room was furnished very plainly with a table and some wooden chairs. The speaker was introduced as a writer named Paul Twitchell. The first thing I noted was that he spoke with a Southern accent. I had always tried to hide my Southern accent because it was put down by my friends. Paul Twitchell, the modern-day founder of Eckankar, acted as if his accent didn't matter.

He asked us to hold our questions until the end of his talk because he was recording it for future use and reference. I was a bit miffed at this. I wanted to argue and question him. I was ready for a knock-down, drag-out battle for spiritual truth.

As the talk went on, I became disappointed because it was clear he was not somebody I could argue with. He simply stated things as truth. He didn't qualify it or quote any holy books. He had no references, no bibliography, nothing.

At the time, that bothered me greatly. How can you assail such a viewpoint? Everyone left, but I kept thinking he had a glimpse of truth. Maybe he could show me how to seek it too. We talked until he offered me a ride home.

I rode home with Paul that night in a yellow, ragtag Volkswagen. Paul was in the driver's seat, and the man who had brought me to the talk was in the front passenger's seat. I sat in the back.

As we were pulling out of the parking lot, I stuck my head between the two front seats and looked at both of them. I asked, "Why do I feel like Arjuna in *The Bhagavad Gita?*" Rebazar (as I later came to know the man in the passenger's seat) laid his head on the window and held his sides with his arms, stomping his feet on the floor and laughing, silently laughing until tears came to his eyes. "Do you know what I mean?" I continued. "I feel like Arjuna—the seeker of God whose chariot was supposedly driven by the reincarnation of God, Krishna!"

On the way home, Rebazar initiated a conversation about the possibility of a Living ECK Master existing on this planet. I said, "No, there's no way I could believe in such a person." Rebazar indicated that the person was not himself, but rather Paul. Somehow, as I looked at Paul, he didn't fit my image of a Godman.

After that discussion, Paul seemed grumpy. He was gruff, short, and terse with his answers. I started to give Paul directions to my house, and he snapped, "I know where you live!"

Stunned, I sat back in my seat and feebly joked, "Home, James." Again the image of Arjuna flitted across my mind. Still, I could not understand it.

Rebazar continued laughing and talking, at ease with himself and Paul's evident discomfort. I couldn't figure Rebazar out and asked how he earned his living. He said, "I build houses." I found it difficult to understand how a carpenter and an intellectual writer would have much in common.

The next thing I knew, a sound filled the air. It was like standing right next to a speeding freight train. The swirling, windlike sound swept me up, and the entire world began spinning. I was above the car, looking down at my weak body in the backseat. Briefly, I tried to remember if I'd drunk anything that evening. I was worried that someone might have slipped me a hallucinogen. I tried to focus my thoughts, but they just faded into a jumble.

When I finally got the strength to turn in my seat and look out the window, I saw there was no road. There was just blackness, with stars. All I could think was, Oh, my God, it's full of stars!

I sat back and thought about what I needed to survive right at that moment. "Air," I decided aloud. "Try to breathe deeply." Then the Sound started again. I heard everything—birds chirping, flutes, and violins—but the strongest sound reminded me of a spaceship being launched. The pressure on my eardrums from these inner sounds was incredible, almost to the point of pain; but it felt good, too. The strange thing was that my outer ears were still picking up the conversation in the car perfectly.

I tried to speak at one point, and it came out sounding like a foreign language. I've got the Holy Spirit, I thought. I'm speaking in tongues. It was funny because I was thinking in English, but it came out in a jumble. I remember Paul took me on a tour of the planets. After seeing the moons of Jupiter, the next thing I knew we were turning onto Sunrise Boulevard, just two or three blocks from my home.

I was pale and in a cold sweat. Literally drenched in sweat, I hadn't a clue as to what was going on. Rebazar was laughing, but gently, gently. We pulled into the driveway, and I moved to jump out. I nearly fell on the pavement because I was so disoriented and weak from the experience. Rebazar looked out the window, and his eyes locked with mine. "I'll see you later," he said.

At that point in my life, Rebazar began appearing in my prayer meditations. He was the first man I wanted to pattern my life after. I learned many spiritual principles through Rebazar in these daily contemplations.

Paul kept in contact with me, too, for awhile. He asked if he could send me letters of encouragement and explanation once a month. But I decided not to study the Eckankar discourses from Paul at that time.

It wasn't until 1977 that I finally made contact with Eckankar. I'd come to a point in my life where nothing seemed right. I sat down one day in deep contemplation and traced my dissatisfaction with life back to that fateful meeting with the bearded man with the strange, flashing eyes. I decided then to embrace Eckankar as my own true path to God.

The experience with these two ECK Masters gave me an unshakable faith in the force of Divine Spirit. It speaks to me today through the Inner Master known as Wah Z, Sri Harold Klemp. Eckankar has given me undeniable strength and knowledge. That's why I'm now in training to be more like these ECK Masters—a spiritual swordsman for the SUGMAD.

12
The Spiritual Exercises of ECKANKAR

The Spiritual Exercises of ECK bring us greater blessings for ourselves and others.

A Spiritual Exercise
for All Religions

Greg Scott

An unusual notice caught my eye one morning as I read a Washington, D. C., newspaper. A spiritual path called Kriya Yoga was putting on a World Conference of Religions.

I clipped the ad and decided to attend. "This path is celebrating the oneness of all religions," I told my wife. "It'll be interesting to see how they perceive Spirit."

I called the phone number on the ad to find out about registration fees. The little notice also said, "Speakers from all paths are invited to come and share the truth of their teachings." I asked the gentleman who answered the telephone, "Is anyone from Eckankar on the program?"

"We called the nearby Eckankar Center several times," he replied, "but no one responded."

"Well, if I happen to be in the area—and I'm not sure yet—I'll be happy to say a few words about Eckankar," I offered. He took my name.

When Friday evening rolled around, I drove home for the weekend, a hundred-mile journey. My wife asked me, "Are you going to that conference in D.C. this weekend?"

It was nearly a two-hundred-mile round-trip. I said, "No way!"

The next morning I awoke with a sure conviction: I had to be at that conference. (Some people receive gentle hints and nudges from Spirit. I felt as if I had been dislodged from my bed by the largest boot in the universe.)

I invited another ECKist to share the journey, and within a few hours we arrived at the conference. As we walked in the door, I told my friend I might be on the program. Sure enough, my name was listed as a speaker. I found the man who organized the event and said, "I just got here. It's 3:30 in the afternoon—I'm sorry if I missed my speaking slot."

He said, "No, you're not going to be on until the evening session."

"What time?"

"Between 4:30 and 8:00 p.m."

"Can you be more specific than that?" I asked.

"Oh, no," he said, "you can only speak when the guru calls you up."

So we went out and ate. Over dinner, my friend and I commented on the guru's broken English. "I hope I know when he's calling me," I joked. We'd also noticed that the guru tended to put each speaker down as he introduced them, explaining their religion so it seemed less than his own.

Just as we walked back in to the conference, I heard the guru announce in perfect English: "And now we will have a presentation on the teachings of Eckankar, which were brought to the attention of modern man by the great ECK Master Sri Paul Twitchell." That was all he said.

I got up on stage and leaned over to the guru. "How long do I have?"

Again the guru addressed the audience. "Greg Scott will tell all he knows about Eckankar in ten minutes."

I said, "That's fine and dandy." None of the previous speakers had talked about the Sound and Light of God, which is the inner voice that guides us as Soul. So I spoke about how to get practical guidance by listening to the various inner Sounds and watching for the inner Light during the Spiritual Exercises of Eckankar.

Just before I stepped down from the stage, the guru turned to me and said, "Well, now, will you explain just one more thing for the audience?"

"What is that?" I asked.

"Will you give them one simple Soul Travel technique?"

"Sure—here's an easy one. Sit quietly and sing this little prayer-song for ten or fifteen minutes: 'HU-U-U (pronounced like the man's name Hugh)...Mahanta (mah-HON-tah).' Sing it softly in a drawn-out breath. Then look gently into the Third Eye between the eyebrows. Watch for an inner Light. It may be a general glow or little blue sparks. It could even look like a beam of light from an open window." The audience chanted HU.

"Next listen for the Sound," I continued softly. "The Music of God can sound like anything from an electrical hum to the piercing, single note of a flute. Or it may come as the voice of your spiritual guide, the Inner Master.

"Spiritual freedom comes when all limits of body, mind, and spirit are dissolved by this Light and Sound

329

of God. Try this exercise each night—you should have results." I left the stage.

The old guru smiled as if that were the only reason he had come.

The Power of HU

Ann Archer Butcher

Sometimes we awake in the morning with a sense that something important has taken place overnight—perhaps through our dreams, we've come to a greater understanding of life. I awoke one morning with just that feeling, and I knew that great blessings were about to come into my life!

I could feel the joy and gratitude growing inside of me and was so moved by this feeling of imminent blessings, I wrote a letter to Eckankar's spiritual leader, Sri Harold Klemp. I mentioned the changes in my life that I could feel coming and thanked him for the inner direction that he provided as the Mahanta, my inner spiritual guide, pointing the way to the greatest good in my life. I put the letter on the dresser in my bedroom and left for a short trip.

That evening as I traveled home with Sarah, my two-year-old daughter, we were hit head-on by a truck. I saw it coming, careening from one side of the highway to the other, then heading straight for us. There was no avoiding it. I turned the wheel sharply so that my

331

sleeping daughter would not take the greatest impact—and called for the help of the ECK Masters.

The truck hit, and I remained conscious. I felt the metal and glass forced against my body. My eyes and mouth were filled with shattered glass, and blood poured down my face and into my ears. I was twisted and smashed and wanted desperately to leave my body and the pain. But more than that, I wanted to listen for Sarah, to know if she were alive.

I could not answer when I heard her tiny voice calling me. But a woman answered, a woman I would later learn was a nursery-school teacher, very adept at helping young children. "Your Mommy is hurt. Do you want to come with me, and we'll go get help? What's your name?"

Sarah told her her name, and they left together, never having spoken to me. I waited and waited for my rescue. I could hear sirens and shouts, but no one approached me.

At last I heard a man ask, "Can you hear me? Can you move?" As I struggled to move the only thing I could, he saw my weak smile and shouted out to the others at the scene, "She's alive!"

"Sorry we didn't get you out of here, honey," he whispered. "We thought we'd already lost you!" were the last words I heard for some time.

When I came to in the operating room, I was sick with pain. I was being tortured! My eyes were being flushed with sharp streams of water while my head was being sewn up. Glass was being removed from my tongue, piece by piece. It was unbearable. One of the doctors was saying that they couldn't use painkillers and warned me not to allow myself to get sick. I was struggling to free my head, and he warned me again. "Hold on; you've got to!"

"Oh, Master," I cried inside myself, "I need you now more than ever!"

As the last piece of glass was removed from my tongue, I weakly whispered, "HU," an ancient name of God, and then shouted it out, "HUUUUUUUU!" Suddenly I heard the nurse encouraging me.

"That's it, sweetheart, you're stabilizing now," she remarked, calling out my vital signs. "Keep it up! You're doing much better," she insisted. Then she joined me in my chant!

"HU," she sang out and then encouraged the others to do the same. The room filled with the sound of "HU," and I could no longer feel the pain. My conscious awareness was outside of my body, and I was feeling quite happy and relaxed, no longer struggling. I smiled.

"Smiling! Can you believe that?" said the doctor who was above my head. "I don't know what you're doing, lady, but keep it up!" he laughed. I promised myself to ask later if this really happened, but I didn't have to. The doctors and nurses in the operating room showed up the next day, inquiring about my "technique." I gladly explained about the power of the HU and the spiritual exercises learned in Eckankar.

And what about Sarah? As soon as possible, they brought her into the operating room and held her above my chest. "Are you OK?" she asked me with a frown.

As I assured her that I would be fine and my face well soon, I could hardly believe my eyes. She looked completely uninjured! "Your bag of clothes got over me, Mom," she informed me, and I understood. My huge laundry bag had been stuffed between the dashboard and the front seat where Sarah was strapped in. It had been forced on top of her during the wreck like a protective cocoon, and though she was sore, she had only a tiny cut on her back.

Much later, when I arrived back at my apartment, I found the letter I had written to Sri Harold lying on my dresser. "Thank you for the great blessings that are about to enter my life," I had written. And I knew as unlikely a blessing as this car wreck might appear to be, it was indeed a blessing. I had been given prior knowledge so there would be no doubt. I wrote a note at the bottom of the letter, explaining briefly what had happened, and mailed it.

At home in bed for weeks, alone, unable to move very much, I was still constantly aware of the blessings pouring into my life. My spiritual insight was growing tremendously. I was getting a much-needed mental and emotional rest. My daughter and her dad were spending a very special time together, and with the pace of my life so different now, I could see everything in a new light.

One day as I lay recuperating, a very special letter arrived. Sri Harold wrote and THANKED ME! He thanked me for being open to the love and protection of the Mahanta, and assured me that I would see the blessings unfold in my life in many ways. And I have!

HU Helps an African Village

Uyi Onaiwu

My village had been wrenched for years by black magic. One of the practitioners was a woman trying to earn the highest rank possible for a female— that of wizard, head of covens.

You see, in my country these things are not hidden as in the West. Her fierce, weird power over the village made it lifeless. Many lost their lives during the dark times, including my grandfather.

As a child, I used to listen to strange sounds and whistles as I lay in bed, but I never connected them with the negative events of that time. The eerie sounds were from the witch's nighttime meetings with familiar spirits. Every so often our leader (the *enogie*, or highest ranking man in the village) would summon his courage to plead with the woman to end these meetings, and they would stop for two or three days.

The hiatus always proved two things: these beings were human, like me; their meetings were the cause of many of our troubles. When they stopped for a while, conditions would improve. I knew I would need the help

335

of a greater power to survive, much less combat, this negative force.

One day, I sat down to sort out the events leading to so many mysterious deaths and departures. I could dimly remember when my mother had first brought me to the village to meet my grandfather. It had been so full of life, with various kinds of sports and festivities, that I didn't want to leave. Now, many villagers were dying of strange illnesses. Others headed for distant places, leaving no one with a love for the town. The few remaining villagers were human, yet not.

After so many attempts by the *enogie* and others to stop this woman, the villagers decided to invite a native doctor to help them. He claimed to be a powerful white wizard who could clean up their homes.

The native man unleashed his power.

During the days that followed, he often commented to me on the strength of the woman's power. At the end of the week, he addressed the people: "I can defeat her, but it will take several years. Even then, it will require a miracle from God. To win the title of wizard, the witch is spreading five or more deadly diseases on the village."

Shortly after this, several children died. The native doctor redoubled his efforts, exhorting the people to help him. They united to fight this evil force and succeeded to a degree. The following week, the woman who had been the source of all the trouble collapsed and died.

I thought happiness would return, but the village remained without life, with only five or six families remaining. Houses started to fall down, and tall grasses overtook the streets.

About this time, I got my first Eckankar discourse

in the mail. Eagerly, I read the monthly lesson. It talked about how to turn a negative situation over to the ECK using the inner vision. I practiced this exercise very faithfully and started saying the sacred name of God, *HU,* as I walked around the village.

Within days, a surprising thing occurred. My father showed up with several of my brothers and a carpenter. They set about repairing the houses and clearing the grasses from the roads. I began to note new signs of life in the people—a few spontaneous smiles—as I chanted HU and helped my brothers.

That night, the Inner Master took me on a dream journey. I was allowed to see the power of the HU. Together, Sri Harold Klemp and I stood in the clearing at the center of the village, listening to the holy sound of HU. A powerful Light—the Light of the ECK— descended in the darkness. Suddenly, whole batches of invisible wizards and witches, who had made our village a center of power, were revealed. They fled to the skies to escape the Light.

Then the future was opened to me. The village would prosper again, full of life, as I remembered it in my youth. I will never forget that dream.

And the dream is coming true. During the past year, many villagers have returned. The town is happy and whole once again—thanks to the incredible power of the HU!

Spiritual Exercise Troubleshooting

Constance Cheong

Sometimes members of Eckankar complain that their minds become distracted while doing the Spiritual Exercises of ECK or that they fall asleep while trying to do them at night. Sound familiar?

I'm sure many of us have experienced this problem, especially when we are very new on the path and not used to sitting down for twenty minutes, looking into the Third Eye at the Inner Master or the Light, and listening to the divine Sound.

When we attempt to put our attention on the Spiritual Exercises of ECK, our minds may wander to the day's activities, problems, fears, and numerous other distractions—in short, everything except the Inner Master. And the more we try to place our attention on Spirit, the more elusive It becomes.

As we become more experienced, we realize we must not force stray thoughts from the mind. We just let them slip away, for the spiritual exercise is most enjoyable when we contain our attention. But this single-mindedness is usually short-lived, for the tug-of-war with unruly thoughts continues until we are able to drive them out effortlessly. I will explain the "effortless effort" in a moment.

First, let me share with you the method I use to stop my mind from wandering. In this confrontation with the Kal, the negative force (for the diversion of attention is obviously the play of the Kal), my mind must be free of all problems and distractions. To ensure this, I do my spiritual exercise at 6:45 a.m. every morning. Doing the exercises at the same time each day helps to condition the mind. It soon learns that this period of time is for spiritual exercises only; other things will be attended to only after the completion of the exercise.

To avoid drowsiness, I make sure I've had plenty of sleep the night before. Then just before I start my spiritual exercise, I do fifteen minutes of physical exercise. This makes me feel refreshed and alert. Then I sit tailor fashion, always in the same corner, and take a few deep breaths to relax.

I begin by visualizing the Inner Master sitting in front of me. Then I look into the Third Eye for the Light and listen for the beautiful Sound Current. I visualize the Inner Master helping me with the spiritual exercises, and together we order the Kal out of our space and enclose our area with four walls and a ceiling.

Then I silently repeat a declaration, such as: I declare myself a channel for the Divine SUGMAD, the ECK, and the Mahanta. Next I thank the SUGMAD (God) for allowing me to return home this lifetime and the Inner Master, the Mahanta, for being with me and guiding me all these years. Last but not least, I thank Divine Spirit for all the spiritual experiences gained.

Then I chant HU (pronounced like the man's name Hugh) or my own secret word, and place my attention on the Third Eye, between the brows and slightly back of the forehead. Here I either visualize the Inner Master or the Light. All the while, I'm listening to the melodious Sound, for I've found that It is the key to keeping my attention focused.

After a while, I lose all awareness of physical surroundings, but the inner voice tells me when the half hour is up. At this point the contemplation has become very enjoyable, so I often continue when time permits.

When I was new on the path, I was not able to see the Light. But by focusing my attention on the Third Eye, listening to the Sound, and chanting HU, I soon learned how. Perseverance is the key. If we keep trying, we will cut down the period of diversion until it is no more.

Now, how to persevere effortlessly? As a new student of ECK, I pondered what made me good at performing something. If a person is good at tennis, speech-making, or organizing, what is it that makes him so? Is it due to the training received, the tools used, or the experience he has accumulated doing it?

I've discovered it is all of those things, plus a love for the activity—a positive attitude that fosters confidence and a sense of purpose.

We have often heard the phrase, *Practice makes perfect*. If we practice placing our attention on the Third Eye, looking for the Light and listening to the Sound, one day we will succeed without effort. It is just like the tennis pro who leaps around the court making impossible shots. He can do it not because of any superhuman qualities, but because he has practiced until the movements are internalized; there is no longer any need for conscious direction.

The practice of keeping the attention focused must become so natural that we succeed without effort. If we make an effort to halt stray thoughts, we will be thinking of them even if they do not enter the mind.

Let me give you an illustration. We usually have no trouble eating. But have you ever shared a meal with someone you were really trying to impress? It is amazing how the food seems to land in your lap, and it is magical how the glass of water tips over. The spiritual exercises are like this. When we just eat normally, it's easy, and when we place our attention on the Inner Master without effort, we simply relax in his presence.

To summarize, spiritual exercises are a matter of discipline and constant practice, until the body and mind learn. It is the love for performing the act and the effort we make to improve ourselves that count. And this should be an effortless effort.

Earth to God, Come In Please...

Joan Klemp

What happens in a Spiritual Exercise of ECK? Essentially you make contact with the Voice of God—the Light and Sound of Divine Spirit Itself!

You may perceive light and/or sounds of the inner planes, the image of the Living ECK Master, or other spiritual travelers. You can receive insights into matters of personal or universal importance. You may visit and learn from the great spiritual travelers, the ECK Masters of the Vairagi. And you can experience the God Worlds and know yourself as Soul, an eternal, individualized spark of the Divine.

One of the most effective Spiritual Exercises of ECK is described by the Living ECK Master, Sri Harold Klemp.

"How can we get the God principle to come to us? Quietly sing this little prayer-song in moments of annoyance or need: 'HU' (pronounced like the man's name Hugh). HU is an age-old name for God.

"Sing 'HU' in a sweet, softly drawn-out breath. Do this at home or even in traffic. In time, you will know what it means to become one with Spirit."

343

Using this spiritual exercise technique, a young woman from Singapore was raised in consciousness to visit one of the higher planes of God. As she began the technique one morning, she heard a humming sound that became louder and louder. She said, "Suddenly, I heard thunder and a loud rush of wind. The wind was blowing very hard. It was like the beginning of a thunderstorm."

Since it was raining, she told herself she would not be able to do her usual morning outdoor physical exercises. Then in her inner vision she saw the Living ECK Master, Harold Klemp. As the image faded away, again she heard loud sounds of thunder and the rushing of winds. But as she opened her eyes and looked out of the window, a quiet and still dawn was breaking.

"There was no storm or wind! It was a bright sunny morning!" she exclaimed. "During my spiritual exercises, I had been taken to the Alakh Lok, which has these sounds, and had been given a beautiful experience in the God Worlds of ECK."

Another member of Eckankar wrote to the Living ECK Master about his inner experiences: "Your image appears in my vision so clearly I think it is almost physical. Yet, this image is very bright, sometimes blue, sometimes white and sunny. With it comes a great release and divine inspiration.

"Lately I also became aware of your voice talking to me within, louder and clearer than ever before. That voice advises me what would be best to do, sometimes before I ask, sometimes only when I shout. You are always with me."

One morning during his spiritual exercise, a man from San Francisco received special insight from another ECK Master, Rebazar Tarzs. Shortly after beginning the Easy Way technique, he entered the Lightning and Moon worlds. Rebazar Tarzs stood on the right side, pointed emphatically toward a large moon, and said, "Gaze upon the moon."

As he gazed, he saw the following message cross the face of the moon: "You are Spirit. God is Spirit. Therefore, you as Spirit are part of God. If you seek knowledge or Light, rely upon your intuitive powers. All the knowledge you need is there within you. Sharpen your intuitive tools. Use your intuitive powers."

He thanked Rebazar Tarzs, for he realized that he had erroneously been led to believe that intuition was not a reliable source of knowledge. "I realized," he said, "that though intuition may not seem at times reliable for material ends, it is always reliable for *spiritual* purposes."

The Living ECK Master will often work with the sincere student through the spiritual exercises to give greater insight and awareness of that individual's own divine potential as Soul. Also at times a greater understanding of the Living ECK Master's function may be given. During a spiritual exercise a young man from Ireland had an experience with the Living ECK Master in some remote place on the inner planes.

"The Living ECK Master," he said, "asked me to step into his shoes." About to do so, the significance of the act struck him, and he hesitated, shy and embarrassed. The Master encouraged him to proceed, saying it was all right.

"When I put them on," he explained, "a very subtle, and at the same time very vivid, feeling came upon me. It was as though there was no left or right, no up or down. The whole universe about me became transparent while still holding form and activity. Everything in it was the same distance away.

"To put it another way, every part of this universe was as accessible in the same way that every part of my physical body is accessible. I felt this great, vast transparency was, in a very subtle sense, a bigger body, except that I did not direct activities. I just observed what was happening in the same way that a father might watch his children playing in the garden. The same sense of responsibility accompanied this experience."

The Living ECK Master many times appears to the spiritual student as a Blue Light. Sometimes it may be gold, white, or other colors. He may be accompanied by other ECK Masters. During her spiritual exercise one day an ECK student said she had the experience of true beingness.

"I expanded in consciousness," she said, "and was brought to a place where I was above the worlds—these worlds comprised my body. All lay within me and were run as if part of me. All flowed from me. I could see and sense a great many Souls striving to catch a glimpse of the Living ECK Master who hovered above all these worlds as a giant blue globe of light and love."

Then she moved on until the worlds no longer involved anything but the feeling "It just is." Suddenly, an enormous white light appeared. "The center of this light drew me into it," she remarked. "I was consumed by the light. I became it. There was only the totality of all. The Sound, or Word of God, was working through me and I had the realization that without me there would be no light. I realized why the Mahanta, the highest of all states of consciousness, is called the Light Giver, the Vi-Guru, or the Light of the World."

After this experience she saw life with new eyes. "I saw the sunlight," she explained, "as the light of the Mahanta—the light in the eyes of every person as the

Mahanta. In fact, our very ability to see and perceive is due to the presence of the Mahanta in these worlds. For without the Mahanta, there would be no light. This experience greatly increased my love for the Living ECK Master."

The great ECK Masters offer a very precious gift to the sincere spiritual seeker; how to make contact with the Voice of God, Divine Spirit Itself. It's up to us whether we accept the gift and use it! What is gained is spiritual knowledge and awareness beyond words.

The Spiritual Exercises of ECK provide a direct linkup with this Light and Sound of God. We can find the answer to any question we may have in our heart— also a sure guidance and protective love we've all but forgotten. When you know *how,* it's as simple as saying, "Earth to God, come in please..."

Glossary

Words set in SMALL CAPS are defined elsewhere in this glossary

ARAHATA. An experienced and qualified teacher for ECKANKAR classes.

CHELA. A spiritual student.

ECK. The Life Force, the Holy Spirit, or Audible Life Current which sustains all life.

ECKANKAR. Religion of the Light and Sound of God. Also known as the Ancient Science of SOUL TRAVEL. A truly spiritual religion for the individual in modern times, known as the secret path to God via dreams and SOUL TRAVEL. The teachings provide a framework for anyone to explore their own spiritual experiences. Established by Paul Twitchell, the modern-day founder, in 1965.

ECK MASTERS. Spiritual Masters who can assist and protect people in their spiritual studies and travels. The ECK Masters are from a long line of God-Realized SOULS who know the responsibility that goes with spiritual freedom.

HU. The most ancient, secret name for God. The singing of the word HU, pronounced like the word *hue,* is considered a love song to God. It is sung in the ECK Worship Service.

INITIATION. Earned by the ECK member through spiritual unfoldment and service to God. The initiation is a private ceremony in which the individual is linked to the Sound and Light of God.

LIVING ECK MASTER. The title of the spiritual leader of ECKANKAR. His duty is to lead SOULS back to God. The Living ECK Master can assist spiritual students physically as the

349

Outer Master, in the dream state as the Dream Master, and in the spiritual worlds as the Inner Master. Sri Harold Klemp became the MAHANTA, the Living ECK Master in 1981.

MAHANTA.   A title to describe the highest state of God Consciousness on earth, often embodied in the LIVING ECK MASTER. He is the Living Word.

PLANES.   The levels of heaven, such as the Astral, Causal, Mental, Etheric, and Soul planes.

SATSANG.   A class in which students of ECK study a monthly lesson from ECKANKAR.

THE SHARIYAT-KI-SUGMAD.   The sacred scriptures of ECKANKAR. The scriptures are comprised of twelve volumes in the spiritual worlds. The first two were transcribed from the inner PLANES by Paul Twitchell, modern-day founder of ECKANKAR.

SOUL.   The True Self. The inner, most sacred part of each person. Soul exists before birth and lives on after the death of the physical body. As a spark of God, Soul can see, know, and perceive all things. It is the creative center of Its own world.

SOUL TRAVEL.   The expansion of consciousness. The ability of SOUL to transcend the physical body and travel into the spiritual worlds of God. Soul Travel is taught only by the LIVING ECK MASTER. It helps people unfold spiritually and can provide proof of the existence of God and life after death.

SOUND AND LIGHT OF ECK.   The Holy Spirit. The two aspects through which God appears in the lower worlds. People can experience them by looking and listening within themselves and through SOUL TRAVEL.

SPIRITUAL EXERCISES OF ECK.   The daily practice of certain techniques to get us in touch with the Light and Sound of God.

SUGMAD.   A sacred name for God. SUGMAD is neither masculine nor feminine; IT is the source of all life.

WAH Z.   The spiritual name of Sri Harold Klemp. It means the Secret Doctrine. It is his name in the spiritual worlds.

How to Take the Next Step
on Your Spiritual Journey

Find your own answers to questions about your past, present, and future through the ancient wisdom of ECKANKAR. Take the next bold step on your spiritual journey.

ECKANKAR can show you why special attention from God is neither random nor only for a few saints. It is for anyone who opens his heart to Divine Spirit, the Light and Sound of God.

Are you looking for the secrets of life and the afterlife? Sri Harold Klemp, today's spiritual leader of ECKANKAR, and Paul Twitchell, its modern-day founder, have written a series of monthly discourses that give unique Spiritual Exercises of ECK. They can lead you in a direct way to God. Those who join ECKANKAR, Religion of the Light and Sound of God, can receive these monthly discourses.

As a Member of ECKANKAR You'll Discover

1. The most direct route home to God through the ECK teachings on the Light and Sound. Plus the opportunity to gain wisdom, charity, and spiritual freedom in this lifetime through the ECK initiations.

2. The spiritual meaning of dreams, Soul Travel techniques, and ways to establish a personal relationship with Divine Spirit through study of monthly discourses. These discourses are for the entire family. You may study them alone at home or in a class with others.

3. Secrets of self-mastery in a Wisdom Note and articles by the Living ECK Master in the *Mystic World,* a quarterly newsletter. In it are also letters and articles from ECK members around the world.

4. Upcoming ECK seminars and other activities worldwide, new study materials from ECKANKAR, and more, in special mailings. Join the excitement. Have the fulfilling experience of attending major ECK seminars!

5. The joy of the ECK Satsang (discourse study) experience in classes and book discussions. Share spiritual experiences and find answers to your questions about the ECK teachings.

How to Find Out More

To request membership in ECKANKAR using your credit card (or for a free booklet on membership) call (612) 544-0066, weekdays, between 8:00 a.m. and 5:00 p.m., central time. Or write to: ECKANKAR, Att: Information, P.O. Box 27300, Minneapolis, MN 55427 U.S.A.

Introductory Books on ECKANKAR

How to Find God,
Mahanta Transcripts, Book 2
Harold Klemp

Learn how to recognize and interpret the guidance each of us is *already receiving* from Divine Spirit in day-to-day events—for inner freedom, love, and guidance from God. The author gives spiritual exercises to uplift physical, emotional, mental, and spiritual health as well as a transforming sound called *HU,* which can be sung for inner upliftment.

ECKANKAR—Ancient Wisdom for Today

Are you one of the millions who have heard God speak to you through a profound spiritual experience? This introductory book will show you how dreams, Soul Travel, and experiences with past lives are ways God speaks to you. An entertaining, easy-to-read approach to ECKANKAR. Reading this little book can give you new perspectives on your spiritual life.

The Spiritual Exercises of ECK
Harold Klemp

This book is a staircase with 131 steps. It's a special staircase, because you don't have to climb all the steps to get to the top. Each step is a spiritual exercise, a way to help you explore your inner worlds. And what awaits you at the top? The doorway to spiritual freedom, self-mastery, wisdom, and love.

Dreams, A Source of Inner Truth
(Audiocassette)

Dreams are windows into worlds beyond the ordinary. This two-tape set can help you open these windows through insights and spiritual exercises given by Sri Harold Klemp, spiritual leader of ECKANKAR.

For fastest service, phone (612) 544-0066 weekdays between 8 a.m. and 5 p.m., central time, to request books using your credit card, or look under **ECKANKAR** in your phone book for an ECKANKAR Center near you. Or write: **ECKANKAR, Att: Information, P.O. Box 27300, Minneapolis, MN 55427 U.S.A.**

There May Be an
ECKANKAR Study Group near You

ECKANKAR offers a variety of local and international activities for the spiritual seeker. With hundreds of study groups worldwide, ECKANKAR is near you! Many areas have ECKANKAR Centers where you can browse through the books in a quiet, unpressured environment, talk with others who share an interest in this ancient teaching, and attend beginning discussion classes on how to gain the attributes of Soul: wisdom, power, love, and freedom.

Around the world, ECKANKAR study groups offer special one-day or weekend seminars on the basic teachings of ECKANKAR. Check your phone book under **ECKANKAR**, or call **(612) 544-0066** for membership information and the location of the ECKANKAR Center or study group nearest you. Or write **ECKANKAR, Att: Information, P.O. Box 27300, Minneapolis, MN 55427 U.S.A.**

☐ Please send me information on the nearest ECKANKAR discussion or study group in my area.

☐ Please send me more information about membership in ECKANKAR, which includes a twelve-month spiritual study.

Please type or print clearly   812

Name _____

Street _____ Apt. # _____

City _____ State/Prov. _____

ZIP/Postal Code _____ Country _____